HOPE BEYOND THE GRAVE

The Christian Story of Death, Resurrection, and Eternal Life

ROBERT GRIFFITH

Copyright © 2025 Grace and Truth Publishing

All rights reserved. No part of this book may be reproduced, stored in a retrieval system, or transmitted in any form, without the written permission of Grace and Truth Publishing.

GRACE AND TRUTH PUBLISHING
P.O. Box 338, Gunnedah NSW 2380 Australia
www.graceandtruthpublishing.com.au

All Bible quotes are from the
NEW INTERNATIONAL VERSION (NIV),
Copyright 1973, 1978 and 1984 by international Bible Society.
Used by permission of Zondervan Publishing House.
All rights reserved.

ISBN 978-1-7642635-2-8

TABLE OF CONTENTS

	Preface	5
1	The Entrance of Death	7
2	What is Death ?	19
3	The Enemy Death – the Victory of the Cross	31
4	The Believers Death: Precious to the Lord	43
5	To Die is Gain: The Intermediate State	55
6	The Metaphor of 'Sleep'	67
7	The Question of 'Soul Sleep'	77
8	The Resurrection of the Dead	83
9	New Heavens and New Earth	93
10	Judgement, Justice and Joy	101
11	Spiritual Death and New Birth	111
12	The Second Death and the Lake of Fire	119
13	Sheol, Hades and Gehenna	129
14	The Death of Death in the Death of Christ	139
15	Grief with Hope: Christian Mourning	149
16	Dying Well: Being Prepared	155
17	Until He Comes: Perseverance	163

Appendix A: Frequently Asked Questions 171
Appendix B: Key Biblical Terms 177
Appendix C: Key Bible Passages 183

PREFACE

This book was not written from a place of academic curiosity or detached theological reflection. It was born in the crucible of grief and forged in the valley of the shadow of death. During the writing of this manuscript, a tragic accident ended the earthly journey of my youngest son, Nicholas, just weeks before his 34th birthday. In the blink of an eye, so much changed. No words can fully describe the depth of sorrow or the agony of absence that has marked each day since then.

Suddenly, all these great themes of life, death, resurrection, and eternity I was writing about were no longer abstract doctrines on a page. They became lifelines for me, and I found myself asking questions I thought I had already answered, crying out for hope with a sense of desperation I had never known before. In those raw and anguished moments, I turned to the Scriptures - not as a theologian or an author, but as a grieving father seeking solid ground beneath my feet.

What I discovered — or rather, rediscovered — was the profound, living hope that Jesus Christ offers in the face of death. A hope that is neither fragile nor sentimental but anchored in the victory of the cross and the reality of the resurrection. A hope that dares to look beyond the grave and see not an end and a closed door, but a glorious beginning and the entrance to glory.

This book is the fruit of that journey. In many ways, it became a letter to myself — a way of processing, praying, and proclaiming what I believe to be true. But it is also my gift to the thousands of others who may be walking this same dark road, asking the same haunting questions, longing for the same eternal assurance.

If you are holding this book in a time of personal loss, or because you are facing the ultimate enemy yourself, I want you to know that you are not alone. The tears on these pages are real, but so is the profound hope and confident assurance you will find here.

Robert Griffith
October 2025

1. THE ENTRANCE OF DEATH

With this singular declaration, the Bible opens not with death, but with life; not with decay, but with beauty: *"In the beginning God created the heavens and the earth."* (Genesis 1:1)

The opening chapters of Genesis reveal a creation shaped by God's wisdom, order, and generosity. Light is called into being, and it is good. Sky, land, and sea are separated and filled. Plants yield fruit. Sun, moon, and stars take their place in the heavens. Living creatures teem in the waters and walk upon the earth. And then, in a stunning, crowning moment of divine intention, *"God created mankind in his own image, in the image of God he created them; male and female he created them."* (Genesis 1:27)

Over and over again, the refrain is repeated: *"And God saw that it was good."* But when the sixth day comes to a close and all the creation stands complete, the language shifts: *"God saw all that he had made, and it was very good."* (Genesis 1:31).

Within that *"very good"* world, there is absolutely no mention of death. There is no funeral, no grief, no disease, no curse. Creation begins with vitality and blessing. God is not a bringer of death, but the Author of life.

Life as the intended design

The biblical account presents human beings as uniquely bearing the image of God — not merely another species among many, but vice-regents, given dominion over creation and called into relationship with the Creator. Genesis chapter 2 draws closer to the creation of humanity, offering a more intimate perspective. *"Then the Lord God formed a man from the dust of the ground and breathed into his nostrils the breath of life, and the man became a living being."* (Genesis 2:7)

This divine breath — not mere biological animation — is what sets human life apart. It is relational, spiritual, and dignified. Man is placed in a garden, not a battlefield. He is given purpose: *"The Lord God took the man and put him in the Garden of Eden to work it and take care of it."* (Genesis 2:15)

He is also given companionship — *"It is not good for the man to be alone."* (Genesis 2:18). Out of Adam, God fashions Eve. Together, they are naked and unashamed. There is no conflict, no shame, no separation. There is only wholeness. This is the world as God intended it to be. A world where humanity lives in harmony with God, with each other, and with the created order. A world in which death is conspicuously absent — not just in experience, but in design. Death, biblically speaking, is not natural in the theological sense. It is not what God called *"very good."* It is not a neutral biological function, but an alien intrusion into a world that was meant for life.

The warning: "You will surely die"

Yet even in paradise, a boundary is drawn. The presence of love requires the possibility of rejection. The presence of obedience implies the possibility of disobedience. And so, God issues a command: *"You are free to eat from any tree in the garden; but you must not eat from the tree of the knowledge of good and evil, for when you eat from it you will certainly die."* (Genesis 2:16-17)

This warning is pivotal. It introduces the concept of death — not as an existing reality, but as a consequence of rebellion. It is the first appearance of death in the Bible, and it comes not as something which is built into creation, but as a threat against it. The Hebrew phrase *"you will certainly die"* is emphatic — literally *"dying you shall die."* It underscores certainty and severity. And yet, there's mystery. What kind of death is God speaking of? Is it instant annihilation? Is it physical? Spiritual? Relational? The full weight of this warning will not really be felt until the boundary is crossed. But already, Scripture is teaching us that death is the result of sin, not the product of biology. It is moral, not merely medical.

The fall: death enters through sin

Genesis 3 is one of the most theologically consequential chapters in the entire Bible. The serpent enters the garden, questioning God's command: *"Did God really say, 'You must not eat from any tree in the garden'?"* (Genesis 3:1).

It is the very first distortion of divine truth. The serpent does not merely tempt with pleasure; he sows real doubt about God's goodness and truthfulness.

Eve responds, quoting the command — but then subtly adds, *"and you must not touch it"* (Genesis 3:3), suggesting a growing sense of distance or distortion. The serpent then offers a direct contradiction: *"You will not certainly die"* (Genesis 3:4). In the face of God's *"you will certainly die,"* the serpent dares to say the opposite. This is more than a lie; it is the foundation of rebellion. At its heart, sin is unbelief — a refusal to trust that God's word is true and good. Humanity will soon learn that unbelief is the foundation of all sin.

So, Adam and Eve eat. Their eyes are opened, but not to godlike glory. Instead, they now can see their nakedness. Shame replaces innocence. They hide. They fear. They shift blame. And then, the inevitable consequences begin to unfold.

God pronounces curses: the serpent is doomed to crawl and eat dust; the woman will suffer pain in childbirth and relational struggle; the man will face toil, frustration, and eventual return to the dust: *"By the sweat of your brow you will eat your food until you return to the ground, since from it you were taken; for dust you are and to dust you will return."* (Genesis 3:19)

Here is the arrival of physical death. The body, formed from the dust and enlivened by the very breath of God, will now decay. Mortality becomes the new reality. Humanity, which was meant to live forever in communion with God, now walks a path that ends in the grave.

But that is not all. Even before the physical return to dust, there is spiritual death — the rupture of fellowship with God. Adam and Eve are banished from the garden, cut off from the tree of life. The cherubim stand guard with a flaming sword. The path back to paradise is closed. Relationship is broken. Humanity is now alive physically but dead spiritually — a tragic inversion of God's original design.

Death defined: separation, not cessation

What is death, then, in the biblical sense? We will explore this more in the next chapter, but for now, death is not merely the end of physical life, but the separation of what was united:

- Physical death is the separation of body and spirit.
- Spiritual death is the separation of the human person from the presence and life of God.
- Relational death appears immediately — blame, shame, hiding, and exile.
- Later on, Scripture will add the second death — eternal separation from God (Revelation 20:14).

Death is therefore always separation, and separation is always tragic, especially when what is being severed was made to be united forever. This is why death is not normal, even though it is universal. We were not made for death. Ecclesiastes says, *"He has also set eternity in the human heart."* (Ecclesiastes 3:11). We grieve death not because we are weak, but because we were created for life.

The spread of death: east of Eden

From the moment Adam and Eve are expelled from Eden, death becomes the new backdrop of the whole human story. The first generation born outside the garden brings the first recorded physical death. But it is not Adam or Eve who dies first — it is Abel, killed by his own brother. *"Now Cain said to his brother Abel, 'Let's go out to the field.' While they were in the field, Cain attacked his brother Abel and killed him."* (Genesis 4:8)

The first human death does not come from natural causes but from violence, underscoring how deeply sin has corrupted the human heart. Cain does not merely sin — he murders. And the Lord confronts him: *"Your brother's blood cries out to me from the ground."* (Genesis 4:10). The ground that once bore fruit in Eden now drinks the blood of the innocent. Death now reigns not just as consequence, but as curse — a shadow over human existence.

Cain is not executed but exiled. He is condemned to wander — a form of living death. This wandering is emblematic of fallen humanity, now estranged from God, neighbour, and home.

The text tells us Cain *"went out from the Lord's presence and lived in the land of Nod, east of Eden."* (Genesis 4:16).

That phrase — *"east of Eden"* — becomes a poetic summary of the human condition: we live in the aftermath of exile, longing for what was lost, bearing the mark of mortality.

In Genesis 5, we read the genealogy from Adam to Noah. It contains a repetitive, solemn drumbeat:

"And then he died."
"And then he died."
"And then he died."

Except for Enoch, who *"walked faithfully with God; then he was no more, because God took him away"* (Genesis 5:24), each name ends with the same refrain. The wages of sin have become the rhythm of history (cf. Romans 6:23).

Death is no longer just a threat; it is now a reality embedded in every generation.

The flood in Genesis 6–9 marks death on a catastrophic scale — not individual mortality but global judgment. In Genesis 6:5 we read, *"Every inclination of the thoughts of the human heart was only evil all the time."* And the Lord grieves.

The world, once declared *"very good,"* now groans under the weight of sin and death. In righteous judgment and merciful preservation, God wipes the slate clean — but not even this cataclysm removes the presence of death.

After the flood, Noah plants a vineyard, gets drunk, and shame reappears. The cycle of death and brokenness continues. What began with a single act of disobedience has now become an inheritance passed from generation to generation — a terrible inheritance of dust and exile.

The protoevangelium: the first glimmer of redemption

However, in the midst of judgment, hope is not extinguished. Even in the pronouncement of the curse, God speaks words of promise.

In Genesis 3:15, directed at the serpent, we read: *"And I will put enmity between you and the woman, and between your offspring and hers; he will crush your head, and you will strike his heel."*

This verse, often called the *protoevangelium* — which is the first gospel — contains the first whisper of redemption. A seed will come from the woman. There will be conflict with evil, but ultimately, the serpent's head will be crushed. Though the heel of the redeemer will be bruised — a picture of suffering — the ultimate victory belongs to the seed of the woman.

Here, even in Genesis, death is not the final word. God is not content to let sin and death reign unchecked. The story of Scripture will now unfold as the story of that promised seed — a story of promise, covenant, incarnation, and resurrection.

This promise reframes how we understand death. Though it remains an enemy, it is now a defeated enemy. Though it reigns in every generation, it does not reign forever. The trajectory of the Bible bends toward resurrection. But that hope will take time to reveal. First, death must be fully exposed for what it is — a thief, a destroyer, a robber of joy.

Throughout the rest of the Bible, death is not spoken of as a friend or a neutral transition. It is consistently portrayed as an enemy. In the clearest terms, Paul declares: *"The last enemy to be destroyed is death."* (1 Corinthians 15:26)

Death is not just a biological process — it is also a theological interruption. It exists because of sin. *"Just as sin entered the world through one man, and death through sin, and in this way death came to all people, because all sinned..."* (Romans 5:12). The biblical worldview ties death to disobedience, not to design.

This is so important to understand. Many in modern theology or philosophy speak of death as natural, even necessary — a kind of cycle of renewal. But Scripture doesn't take that view.

From God's perspective, death is not a necessity — it's a tragedy. God does not delight in the death of the wicked (Ezekiel 18:23). Jesus weeps at Lazarus's tomb (John 11:35), even knowing He is about to raise him. Why? Because death, even when reversed, is still grievous. It is a violation of God's original intent.

This is what makes the gospel so staggering. God does not merely explain death; He enters into it. In Christ, the Creator submits to His own curse in order to break it. *"Since the children have flesh and blood, he too shared in their humanity so that by his death he might break the power of him who holds the power of death — that is, the devil."* (Hebrews 2:14).

The one who is life became obedient to death (Philippians 2:8). Why? So that death might die. So that humanity might live again. So that the story which began in a garden of life, shattered by sin, might one day end in a city where there is no more death. (Revelation 21:4).

Framing our journey ahead

As we begin this exploration of death, we must hold tightly to this foundational truth: death was not part of God's original design. It is not a teacher, not a friend, not a doorway in any romanticized sense. It is an invader. And yet, it is an invader whose days are numbered. In this chapter we have traced the origin of death:

- God created a world of life, goodness, and harmony.
- Human disobedience introduced death — physical, spiritual, relational.
- That death spread to all people, and with it came grief, violence, and exile.
- But even in the moment of judgment, God spoke a word of promise — a coming redeemer.

In the chapters ahead, we will explore what happens after death — what it means to die in Christ, what the intermediate state is, what resurrection will look like. We will also consider spiritual death, the second death, and the living hope that marks the Christian vision of eternity. But it all begins here: in the garden, where death first entered — not as friend, but as a thief.

Theological depth: defining death as separation

Throughout Scripture, death is never reduced to mere physical cessation. It is always more — a condition, a state of separation, a sign of disunity. When Adam and Eve were told, *"you will certainly die,"* the effects were not limited to biology. Their immediate experience was alienation — from God, from each other, and from the created world.

Theologians across centuries have recognized this layered nature of death. Augustine wrote of *"disordered loves"* as the mark of fallen humanity — not just a disruption of affections, but of design. Calvin, in his Institutes, declared that *"death is not the natural end of man, but the punishment for sin, and hence a token of God's wrath."* This understanding permeates Scripture: death is exile, not release.

Biblically, we can identify three primary forms of death:

1. *Physical Death* — the separation of the soul from the body (Genesis 3:19; Ecclesiastes 12:7; Hebrews 9:27).
2. *Spiritual Death* — the separation of the person from God due to sin (Ephesians 2:1; Isaiah 59:2).
3. *The Second Death* — the eternal separation from God in judgment (Revelation 20:14; 21:8).

Each form of death is a rupture. None are what God originally intended. Even the *"sleep"* metaphor so often used in the New Testament to describe physical death, only makes sense because it anticipates awakening. The dead in Christ are not obliterated — they are at rest, awaiting resurrection. It is the resurrection, not death, that is our hope.

In our modern world, death is often sanitized or euphemized. People "pass away," "move on," or are "lost." Even in Christian circles, death is sometimes treated as a gentle transition, a home-going, a spiritual migration. While there is truth in the comfort that believers are with Christ, we must be really careful we don't domesticate death.

Jesus really wept at the tomb of Lazarus, even though He knew resurrection was minutes away. He was *"deeply moved in spirit and troubled."* Why? Because death is a foreign intruder into God's good creation. Its presence is offensive, and while it will be undone, it must first be named for what it is: the last enemy.

Death and the human experience

Our entire existence takes place in the aftermath of the Fall. We are born into a world where death reigns — but our hearts do not accept it easily. As C.S. Lewis observed, *"It is hard to have patience with people who say 'There is no death,' or 'Death doesn't matter.' There is death. And whatever is matters. And whatever happens has consequences, and it and they are irrevocable and irreversible."*

Even the most secular hearts mourn death as a violation. We dress the body. We gather in silence. We say things like, *"It's not fair,"* or *"She was taken too soon."* Even those who don't believe in Eden, still long for it. Even when they deny God, they protest against His absence. The ache we feel in the face of death is not simply sorrow at a biological fact — it is the soul crying out against injustice.

Ecclesiastes says, *"God has set eternity in the human heart."* (Ecclesiastes 3:11). This is why we find death unnatural, even though it happens to everyone. This is why grief feels like protest. We were made for life, not for endings. Death confronts us with our finitude, but it also confronts us with our origin — we were not meant to die. And yet, because of sin, we do. Romans 5:12 says, *"Sin entered the world through one man, and death through sin, and in this way, death came to all people, because all sinned."*

Paul doesn't say that death entered through biology, but through sin. And this is why every gospel-centred theology of death must begin where Paul begins: with Adam, with disobedience, and with the spread of death as both condition and consequence. But Paul doesn't stop there. In the same chapter, he points forward: *"Just as sin reigned in death, so also grace might reign through righteousness to bring eternal life through Jesus Christ our Lord."* (Romans 5:21)

Grace does not simply match death; it actually overcomes it. Righteousness is not just for the afterlife; it is life itself. Christ, the second Adam, comes not merely to repair the breach, but to resurrect the dead.

Christ and the entrance into death

The most astonishing aspect of biblical theology is not that death is the enemy — that is intuitive. What's astonishing is that God Himself, in Christ, enters into death to destroy it from within. Hebrews 2:14-15 says: *"Since the children have flesh and blood, he too shared in their humanity so that by his death he might break the power of him who holds the power of death — that is, the devil — and free those who all their lives were held in slavery by their fear of death."*

Fear of death is a form of slavery. It chains humanity to anxiety, violence, denial, and despair. But the incarnation changes the equation. The Son of God becomes mortal. He is *"obedient to death — even death on a cross."* (Philippians 2:8). In Gethsemane, He faces the weight of sin and its consequences. On the cross, He cries out in forsakenness. And in the tomb, He enters the silence of death.

But death cannot hold Him. Acts 2:24 says, *"God raised him from the dead."* Resurrection is not resuscitation — it is the beginning of a whole new creation. Christ rises not as a ghost, not as a disembodied soul, but with a glorified body, the first fruits of what is to come (1 Corinthians 15:20).

This is the gospel's answer to the problem of death. Not escape, but victory. Not consolation, but conquest.

Why this really matters

Everything we believe about life, grief, hope, and eternity is shaped by how we understand death. If death is natural, then grief is futile. If death is an illusion, then resurrection is unnecessary. But if death is an enemy — a real enemy — then resurrection is essential. And if resurrection is real, then hope is stronger than grief. We mourn deeply, but not as those without hope. We plan funerals not just as farewells, but as acts of protest and faith — proclaiming that this body, laid in the earth, is not the end. That *"the dead in Christ will rise first"* (1 Thess. 4:16). That Christ's tomb is empty. That every grave in Him will one day be empty too.

Understanding death rightly grounds our theology in realism and grace. It enables us to be honest about sorrow without collapsing into despair. It frames our gospel with clarity: the problem was death, and the solution was Christ. The church does not flinch in the face of death. It sings. It grieves. It waits. It hopes. Paul puts it this way in 2 Timothy 1:10: *"Christ Jesus... has destroyed death and has brought life and immortality to light through the gospel."* That is the message we must carry — as pastors, as teachers, as believers, as those who have stood at gravesides and wondered what comes next.

Closing reflection: between dust and glory

The Bible begins with life — breath, blessing, and beauty. Death enters not by divine design, but by human rebellion. It spreads, corrupts, devours. And yet, from the very beginning, God speaks a promise — a redeemer will come. Christ fulfils that promise not by avoiding death but by entering it. And in His rising, He transforms it. For those in Christ, death is no longer a black hole but a doorway — not into nothingness, but into the presence of the Lord, and one day into bodily resurrection and new creation. This is where we begin our journey. With eyes wide open to the reality of death — but hearts firmly anchored in the victory of Christ. With tears that fall honestly — and a hope that rises defiantly. With dust in our hands — and glory in our future.

2. WHAT IS DEATH?

What is death? Let's dig a little deeper to answer this question. The word itself evokes sorrow, mystery, and even fear. Yet in Scripture, death is not a vague or undefined term. It is a multi-faceted reality — not just an event, but a condition. It touches not only the body, but also the soul, the spirit, and, ultimately, the eternal destiny of each person. To build a theology of death grounded in Scripture, we must understand the categories it uses. As noted in chapter 1, the Bible speaks of death in three main ways: physical death, spiritual death, and the second death. Each is distinct yet connected, and each is absolutely critical for understanding the Christian hope of life, resurrection, and redemption.

Physical death: the separation of body and spirit

The most familiar form of death is physical. It is the moment life ceases, when breath stops, the heart stills, and the body begins to return to the earth from which it came. The Bible consistently refers to physical death as the separation of body and spirit. In Genesis 3:19, after the Fall, God says to Adam: *"By the sweat of your brow you will eat your food until you return to the ground, since from it you were taken; for dust you are and to dust you will return."*

This is the first explicit reference to physical death as a direct consequence of sin. The body, made from dust, will decay and return to the dust. Death was not built into humanity's design — it was the result of disobedience. God did not create humans to die; He created them to live in communion with Him. Death is not a neutral biological process but the penalty for sin.

Later Scriptures reinforce this understanding. Ecclesiastes 12:7 captures the moment of death this way: *"...and the dust returns to the ground it came from, and the spirit returns to God who gave it."* Here, the essence of physical death is described in relational terms — the body returns to the ground, and the spirit returns to God. Death is not annihilation. It is separation. James 2:26 offers a concise theological definition: *"The body without the spirit is dead..."*

This clear statement reflects the consistent biblical anthropology: the human person is a unity of body and spirit. Death divides what God joined. It is unnatural, in the deepest theological sense. Human beings were not meant to be disembodied spirits or decaying flesh. The original design was holistic life — animated by God's breath, dwelling in God's presence, sustained in relational unity. Death breaks that unity.

Throughout the Old Testament, physical death is often spoken of with solemnity. Patriarchs are *"gathered to their people"* or *"rest with their ancestors."* (Genesis 25:8; 2 Kings 22:20). Yet even these phrases are filled with longing. The burial of loved ones — in tombs, caves, or ancestral lands — was not just about tradition. It reflected a hope, however dim, that death was not the end of the story.

In the New Testament, Jesus Himself affirms the reality and grief of physical death. At the tomb of Lazarus, though He knows resurrection is moments away, He weeps (John 11:35). The crowd notices: *"See how he loved him!"* Jesus does not treat death casually. Even though He will conquer it, He acknowledges it as a real enemy. This matters. The Son of God does not call death a friend. He stands before it with holy grief.

Spiritual death: the separation of the soul from God

While physical death is certainly the most visible and universally acknowledged, the Bible places an even greater emphasis on spiritual death — that is, the inward, present condition of being separated from God due to sin. Paul describes it vividly in Ephesians 2:1: *"As for you, you were dead in your transgressions and sins..."* This does not mean the Ephesian believers had stopped breathing or living biologically. Rather, they were spiritually dead — alienated from the life of God. To be spiritually dead is to be alive in body but cut off from divine fellowship. It is a death of the soul, a condition of inner exile.

The first sign of spiritual death appears In Genesis chapter 3, immediately after Adam and Eve sin. Though they are still physically alive, their relationship with God is broken.

They hide. They are afraid. They are expelled from the garden. The communion they enjoyed with their Creator is severed. This is the essence of spiritual death. Isaiah 59:2 puts it plainly: *"But your iniquities have separated you from your God; your sins have hidden his face from you, so that he will not hear."*

This language of separation runs like a thread through the biblical description of spiritual death. It is not a passive state but a relational rupture. God is life. To be separated from Him is to be in death — even while breathing, working, and walking.

Jesus alludes to this kind of death in Luke 15 in His parable of the prodigal son. When the son returns, the father says: *"For this son of mine was dead and is alive again; he was lost and is found."* The son had not died physically. But his rebellion and departure from the father's house had placed him in a kind of living death — isolated, disoriented, enslaved to sin. His restoration is described in terms of resurrection: *"He was dead and is alive again."*

John 5:24 offers one of the most hopeful declarations about spiritual death and life: *"Whoever hears my word and believes him who sent me has eternal life and will not be judged but has crossed over from death to life."*

The spiritual death caused by sin is not irreversible. Through faith in Jesus Christ, one can 'cross over' – from separation to communion, from exile to adoption, from darkness to light. Paul speaks of this transformation in Colossians 2:13: *"When you were dead in your sins... God made you alive with Christ."*

This is the miracle of regeneration — spiritual resurrection in the present, as a foretaste of the physical resurrection to come.

Understanding spiritual death is critical, especially in a culture where morality is too often measured by action rather than relationship. People may be generous, kind, or religious, yet still dead in sin if they are not reconciled to God. The gospel is not about making good people better. It is about bringing dead people to life.

The second death: eternal separation from God

The most sobering category of death in the Bible is what Revelation calls *"the second death."* Unlike physical and spiritual death — which are temporal and, in Christ, reversible — the second death is final and eternal. Revelation 20:14-15 offers a clear definition: *"Then death and Hades were thrown into the lake of fire. The lake of fire is the second death. Anyone whose name was not found written in the book of life was thrown into the lake of fire."*

The second death is not mere extinction. It is actually the eternal separation of the unrepentant from God's presence, mercy, and blessing. While Scripture uses symbolic language for judgment (fire, outer darkness, weeping), the underlying reality is just terrifying — a permanent condition of estrangement from God.

This is the end result of spiritual death when left unredeemed. If spiritual death is separation from God now, the second death is separation from God forever. It is what awaits those who resist the grace of Christ and persist in rebellion.

Jesus speaks of this judgment in Matthew 10:28: *"Do not be afraid of those who kill the body but cannot kill the soul. Rather, be afraid of the One who can destroy both soul and body in hell."* Here, death is not just what happens to the body. The soul, too, can face destruction — not in the sense of ceasing to exist, but in being excluded from the life of God.

Paul writes of this fate in 2 Thessalonians 1:9: *"They will be punished with everlasting destruction and shut out from the presence of the Lord and from the glory of his might."* Notice again the language of separation — *"shut out from the presence of the Lord."*

The horror of the second death is not merely torment; it is abandonment. It is what happens when one chooses to remain spiritually dead and finally rejects the life offered in Christ. Yet even here, the Gospel stands as a barrier. Revelation 2:11 gives this promise to the one who overcomes: *"The one who is victorious will not be hurt at all by the second death."*

This is the ultimate hope: those who belong to Jesus Christ will experience neither eternal separation nor eternal judgment. They will face physical death, perhaps, but not the second death. For them, death has been swallowed up in victory.

The unity of death: one root, three branches

The three forms of death in Scripture — physical, spiritual, and the second death — may appear distinct, but they all spring from the same root: sin. They are not separate phenomena, but interconnected consequences of the Fall, revealing the depth and reach of humanity's rebellion against God. At the heart of this biblical framework is a simple but profound truth: to be cut off from God is to be dead, in any and every sense. He alone is life. He alone gives breath, sustains creation, and redeems what is broken. Therefore, all death — whether of body, soul, or future — flows from a rupture in relationship with Him.

We can think of these three forms of death as past, present, and future for the unredeemed person:

- Spiritual death is the present reality of those who are alienated from God by sin (Ephesians 2:1).
- Physical death is the inevitable outcome in this fallen world — the future all inherit biologically (Hebrews 9:27).
- The second death is the final destiny of those who remain unreconciled — the eternal judgment beyond the grave (Revelation 20:14).

Yet for every believer, each form of death is confronted and overcome in the gospel.

TYPE	ORIGIN	BIBLICAL DESCRIPTION	CONQUERED BY
Spiritual death	Sin in the soul	Separation from God (Eph. 2:1)	New birth in Christ (John 5:24)
Physical death	Sin in the body	Separation of soul and body (Gen. 3:19)	Resurrection (1 Cor. 15:52)
Second death	Final judgment	Eternal separation (Rev. 20:14)	Security in Christ (Rev. 2:11)

This theological map helps us see that death is not just an event at the end of life — it is a spiritual condition, a biological certainty, and, apart from grace, an eternal peril. But through Christ, life replaces death at every level.

The cross and the defeat of every death

Christ's redemptive work addresses each of these dimensions of death — decisively, personally, and eternally. Only through the cross and resurrection can death be not just delayed or softened, but defeated.

Christ conquers spiritual death through regeneration

When Jesus speaks to Nicodemus in John 3, He does not begin by addressing future judgment. He speaks of the need for new birth now: *"Very truly I tell you, no one can see the kingdom of God unless they are born again."*

This rebirth is spiritual resurrection, the reversal of Ephesians 2:1 — the movement from being *"dead in transgressions"* to being *"made alive with Christ"* (Colossians 2:13). This is not self-improvement; this is divine intervention. Only God can raise the spiritually dead.

This is why the gospel is not about moral effort. It is about spiritual transformation. When a person believes in Christ, they cross over from death to life (John 5:24). This crossing is not symbolic. It is regeneration of the spirit, resurrection of the soul, the restoration of fellowship with God, the end of alienation, and the beginning of eternal life.

Christ conquers physical death through His resurrection

On the third day after the crucifixion, Jesus rose bodily from the grave. This was not a private vision or a ghostly experience. The tomb was empty. The linen wrappings were left behind. The risen Christ appeared, ate, spoke, and bore the wounds of the cross. Paul calls Him *"the first fruits of those who have fallen asleep."* (1 Corinthians 15:20). His resurrection is not just proof of life after death — it is the prototype of what is to come.

Just as Adam's sin brought death to all, Christ's resurrection brings life to all who are in Him. *"For as in Adam all die, so in Christ all will be made alive."* (1 Corinthians 15:22). Physical death is still present in the world, even for believers. But its power is broken. Its permanence is revoked. The resurrection of Christ is a down payment on our future resurrection. We grieve at death, yes, but not as those without hope (1 Thessalonians 4:13-14). Christ has taken away death's sting (1 Corinthians 15:55).

Christ conquers the second death by substitution

The most profound and terrifying judgment in Scripture is the second death — the lake of fire, the place of separation from God's glory and grace. And yet, for those who belong to Christ, this fate is no longer a threat. Why? Because Christ endured the full weight of divine judgment in our place.

On the cross, He bore the wrath of God — not just physical agony, but spiritual abandonment. He cried out, *"My God, my God, why have you forsaken me?"* (Matthew 27:46). In that cry, we hear the sound of the second death being absorbed by the only One who did not deserve it. As Paul writes: *"God made him who had no sin to be sin for us, so that in him we might become the righteousness of God."* (2 Corinthians 5:21)

The second death holds no power over those whose names are written in the Lamb's book of life. They are secure — not because of their merit, but because of Christ's substitution. *"The one who is victorious will not be hurt at all by the second death."* (Revelation 2:11). This is the good news: Christ has conquered death in all its forms. The gospel is not merely about going to heaven. It is about being made alive now, rising again then, and living forever — all through the victory of Jesus.

Pastoral implications: preaching, counselling, and grieving

Understanding the multi-dimensional nature of death can have profound pastoral implications. It shapes how we preach, how we grieve, how we counsel, and how we proclaim hope in a dying world.

Preaching the full gospel

Many sermons speak of eternal life without clarifying what kind of death Christ overcomes. But the power of the gospel shines brightest when we understand the depth of the problem. To tell someone *"Jesus loves you and gives you life"* carries far greater weight when the reality of spiritual death, physical decay, and eternal judgment is clearly understood.

The preacher's task is not to make death less frightening by sentimentalizing it, but to proclaim its defeat through Christ. When people see what they are being saved from — and what they are being saved to — the cross becomes not just a doctrine, but a lifeline.

Grieving with Biblical understanding

Christian funerals are moments of unique tension. We grieve deeply, yet we also hope defiantly. If we truly understand that physical death is temporary, spiritual death is reversible, and the second death is avoidable — then we can mourn with hope and comfort the sorrowful with truth.

It is right to cry, to ache, to feel the void of loss. But it is also right to proclaim that death is not the final word. The person who dies in Christ has not ceased to exist. They are with the Lord now — and they will be raised bodily at His return. This is not poetic comfort; it is theological reality.

Counselling the spiritually dead

Many people in our churches are physically alive but spiritually dead. They may attend regularly, serve faithfully, and speak respectfully — yet they have never crossed over from death to life. Understanding spiritual death helps us diagnose the real issue: not bad behaviour, but lack of regeneration.

Evangelism is not about convincing good people to try harder. It is about calling dead people to life in Christ. Our message is not self-help. It is resurrection.

Living with eternal urgency

Finally, understanding the second death reminds us that eternity is not optional. Every person we meet is heading toward one of two destinies: eternal communion or eternal separation. This is not a fear tactic — it is biblical truth. And it should drive us to pray, to preach, and to live with urgency.

The victory of Christ over death must not make us complacent — it must make us compassionate. We are bearers of the only message that turns graves into gateways and judgment into joy.

Resurrection and the undoing of death

If death is separation, then resurrection is reunion. It is the total reversal of all that was broken by sin. Just as Christ conquered death in all its dimensions — spiritual, physical, and eternal — the resurrection of the dead will restore everything sin fractured.

In 1 Corinthians 15, Paul offers the most extended treatment of resurrection in Scripture. He insists that the resurrection is not a metaphor or spiritual uplift, but a bodily reality, grounded in the resurrection of Jesus Himself: *"But Christ has indeed been raised from the dead, the first fruits of those who have fallen asleep. For since death came through a man, the resurrection of the dead comes also through a man."* (1 Corinthians 15:20-21)

This means that physical death is not permanent. Our bodies will be raised — not merely reanimated but transformed. Paul uses the metaphor of a seed: *"What is sown is perishable, what is raised is imperishable."* The body that dies is not discarded but renewed. The new body is real, physical, and immortal — designed and destined for eternity.

This bodily resurrection is the full undoing of physical death. It is the reunion of body and spirit in glorified wholeness. In this way, the separation caused by death is reversed completely. But the resurrection also signals the final end of spiritual and eternal death. Revelation 20:14-15 tells us that at the final judgment, *"death and Hades were thrown into the lake of fire."*

In other words, death itself dies. Its power, its sting, its claim — all are extinguished. And for those whose names are written in the Lamb's book of life, there is no second death. Revelation 21:4 gives the ultimate promise: *"He will wipe every tear from their eyes. There will be no more death or mourning or crying or pain, for the old order of things has passed away."*

What begins in Genesis, with separation, shame, exile, and mortality, wonderfully ends in Revelation with life, communion, and permanence. The tree of life reappears (Revelation 22:2), not in a garden now, but in a city — a resurrected creation for resurrected people. In Christ, death is not just postponed. It is reversed. Not just resisted — but overthrown. The resurrection is not a footnote in Christian doctrine; it is the hinge of history, the guarantee that all forms of death have a divine expiration date.

Why our definition of death shapes our definition of life

Understanding death biblically also helps us recover a richer understanding of life. In a world shaped by mortality, we tend to define life biologically — the ability to breathe, move, think, feel, act. But Scripture defines life not merely as existence, but as relationship with God.

In John 17:3, Jesus says: *"Now this is eternal life: that they know you, the only true God, and Jesus Christ, whom you have sent."* Life is not simply the opposite of death in physical terms. It is fellowship with the Source of life. This means that a person can be physically healthy, socially successful, and intellectually brilliant — and still be dead, spiritually speaking.

Conversely, a person who is dying of illness, cut off from society, and forgotten by the world can be truly alive if they are in Christ. Life is not measured by duration or sensation but by communion with God. This redefinition matters immensely. It reorients our priorities. If life is knowing God, then the pursuit of life becomes the pursuit of holiness, intimacy with Christ, and the indwelling of the Holy Spirit. It also clarifies our mission: we are not just preserving life, but offering it — the real, eternal kind.

It also means that the Christian vision of life is deeply relational. Death is separation; life is union — with God, with His people, with creation in its redeemed form. The gospel is not just good news that we won't perish, but that we will truly live — now and forever.

Living in the light of death's defeat

A biblical understanding of death — in all its forms — not only informs our theology; it transforms our daily lives. Christians are not called to deny death, nor to obsess over it, but to live in its shadow with defiant hope. Because death has been defeated, we can now:

Live without fear

Hebrews 2:15 tells us that Jesus came to *"free those who all their lives were held in slavery by their fear of death."* This fear enslaves — it drives anxiety, obsession with youth, denial of aging, and panic at loss. But the Christian no longer needs to be afraid. Death has become, in Christ, not a wall but a door. We do not minimize its pain — but we do not submit to its tyranny. Paul writes, *"To live is Christ and to die is gain."* This is not bravado; it is resurrection logic. If Christ has overcome, so will we.

Grieve with hope

1 Thessalonians 4:13 says, *"Brothers and sisters, we do not want you to be uninformed about those who sleep in death, so that you do not grieve like the rest of mankind, who have no hope."* Grief is not forbidden — but despair is overcome by knowledge. We know the resurrection is coming. We know the dead in Christ are not lost, but secure. This changes how we mourn.

Evangelise with urgency

If spiritual and eternal death are real, then our task as witnesses is urgent. We are not simply inviting people to church. We are inviting them to pass from death to life. Evangelism is not persuasion — it is actually participation in resurrection. And our confidence is not in our eloquence, but always in the power of the gospel.

Die with dignity

Christians do not romanticize death — but neither do we fear it as a final defeat. Many faithful believers throughout history have faced death with courage, peace, and even joy. Their testimony is not sentimental but grounded in the reality that death has lost its sting. Dying well is part of living well. Preparing our hearts, our families, and even our churches for how we face death is part of Christian discipleship. To die in Christ is not to be defeated, but to be welcomed. More on dying well in chapter 16.

Conclusion

To name death rightly is to understand it biblically — not as fate, friend, or illusion, but as enemy, defeated by Christ. Physical death will come to us all. Spiritual death came to us all — but for those in Christ, it has been replaced with new life. And the second death has no claim on those whose names are written in the Lamb's book.

Death is separation. Life is union. Sin creates the breach. Christ restores the bond. And so, we proclaim, with Paul: *"Death has been swallowed up in victory. Where, O death, is your victory? Where, O death, is your sting?"*

This is not the language of theory. It is the cry of triumph. The believer does not merely escape death — he overcomes it. And that victory, given freely by grace, becomes the lens through which we live, grieve, serve, and hope.

The world is still full of dying things. But the church is full of people made alive — people who were dead and now live. And one day soon, that life will shine across all creation. The final death will die. And the sons and daughters of God will rise, incorruptible.

Until then, we do not shrink back. We name death for what it is — and we name Jesus as the One who defeated it.

3. THE ENEMY DEATH AND THE VICTORY OF THE CROSS

In a world accustomed to death, there is a strange temptation to treat it as something normal, even friendly. Philosophers have called it the great equalizer. Poets have imagined it as a gentle release. Modern secularism has often reframed death as just a biological inevitability, devoid of moral or theological weight. Even within Christian circles, sentiment sometimes replaces Scripture, turning death into a gateway to peace or *"just part of life."* But, as we have seen, the Bible speaks very differently.

The Apostle Paul describes death as our enemy which must be destroyed. Jesus weeps at death's presence, even as He prepares to reverse it (John 11:35). Revelation describes death and Hades being thrown into the lake of fire (Revelation 20:14). Scripture consistently treats death not as a friend to be embraced, but as a hostile power that entered the world through sin, reigned over humanity like a tyrant, and required nothing less than the death of the Son of God to defeat it.

This chapter explores how death, introduced as a consequence of sin, is personified in Scripture as a vicious enemy — and how the victory of the cross secures the beginning of its end. The Christian hope does not pretend death away. It proclaims death's defeat.

Death is an enemy, not a design

In 1 Corinthians 15, Paul is offering a sweeping defence of the bodily resurrection. In doing so, the Apostle frames death in unmistakably adversarial terms. As he describes the end of all things — the return of Christ, the resurrection of the dead, the consummation of God's kingdom — he includes this striking statement: *"The last enemy to be destroyed is death."* (v.26) This is not a poetic flourish. It is a theological assertion. Death is an enemy. It is not a friend in disguise, not a stage of transformation, not a neutral transition. It is an invader, a vandal, a thief. It Is the final frontier of all that sin has broken.

This claim is rooted in the earliest pages of Scripture. As we saw in Chapter 1, God created a world without death. Life, not death, was the hallmark of Eden. The breath of God filled Adam's lungs. Communion with the Creator sustained Adam and Eve. It was sin, not creation, that brought death into the human story. Romans 5:12 makes this explicit: *"Therefore, just as sin entered the world through one man, and death through sin, and in this way death came to all people, because all sinned."*

Death is not a design feature. It is a malfunction caused by rebellion. It is not natural in the theological sense. We were not meant to die. We were made to live — in bodies, in communion, in the presence of God. Death is the undoing of that design.

Even when Scripture uses softer metaphors for death, such as "sleep," it does so with a view to resurrection. It is sleep only in the sense that it is temporary for those in Christ. But it is still an enemy, and enemies are not meant to be normalized. They are meant to be defeated.

Christ's death as victory, not defeat

It would be natural to assume that if death is the great enemy, then the crucifixion of Jesus — His death — must be its greatest victory, and, on the surface, that is exactly what it appears to be. The sinless Son of God is mocked, tortured, and executed. His body is broken. His breath ceases. He is buried in a borrowed tomb.

To the watching world, this looks like the triumph of death. The Word became flesh — and the flesh was torn, drained, and then brutally silenced. But Scripture reveals a deeper truth. The cross is not the moment when death won. It is the moment when death was undone from within.

Hebrews 2:14-15 says it plainly: *"Since the children have flesh and blood, he too shared in their humanity so that by his death he might break the power of him who holds the power of death – that is, the devil – and free those who all their lives were held in slavery by their fear of death."*

This stunning paradox is at the core of Christian theology: death was defeated by dying. The One who had no sin bore the full consequence of sin. He entered into death not as a victim, but as a conqueror. He submitted to it temporarily in order to break its hold permanently.

On the cross, Jesus did not just suffer physically. He experienced the full curse of death — the full weight of divine wrath, the abandonment symbolized in His cry: *"My God, my God, why have you forsaken me?"* (Matthew 27:46). This was not just the pain of mortality; it was the agony of sin's full consequence. He bore our guilt. He absorbed our separation. And in doing so, He disarmed death of its power.

Colossians 2:13-15 echoes this victory: *"He forgave us all our sins, having cancelled the charge of our legal indebtedness… He took it away, nailing it to the cross. And having disarmed the powers and authorities, He made a public spectacle of them, triumphing over them by the cross."* Death's power is legal and spiritual — it reigns because of sin, because of guilt, because of condemnation. But the cross removes guilt. It cancels condemnation. And with it, the very foundation of death's authority is broken.

The resurrection: proof of victory

If the cross is the victory, then the resurrection is the proof. Without it, the cross might still appear as a tragedy. But with it, the cross becomes the ultimate triumph.

Paul writes in Romans 6:9: *"For we know that since Christ was raised from the dead, he cannot die again; death no longer has mastery over him."* The resurrection is not a reversal … it is a proclamation. It says to the world: death lost. The grave could not hold Him. The penalty is paid, the power is broken, and the future is changed. Christ's resurrection is not an isolated event. It is the beginning of a new creation. Paul calls it *"the first fruits of those who have fallen asleep."* (1 Corinthians 15:20). Just as the first fruits in an agricultural setting guarantee the full harvest, so Christ's rising guarantees that all who belong to Him will rise.

His victory is not private. It is ours by union with Him. As Paul declares in 2 Timothy 1:10: *"...our Saviour, Christ Jesus, who has destroyed death and has brought life and immortality to light through the gospel."* This is not poetic exaggeration. It is theological fact. Christ has destroyed death — not in the sense that people no longer die physically, but in the sense that death no longer has the final word.

For the believer, death is no longer a prison. It is a hallway. It is no longer our master. It is a defeated foe, humiliated by the resurrection of the Lord of life.

Victory through substitution

How did this victory come to us? The answer is found in one of the most important doctrines of the Christian faith: substitution. Christ did not simply defeat death by example or force. He defeated it by taking our place under its curse. He did not just overcome death — He endured it for us.

Isaiah 53:5 speaks of the Suffering Servant: *"He was pierced for our transgressions, he was crushed for our iniquities... and by his wounds we are healed."* 2 Corinthians 5:21 adds: *"God made him who had no sin to be sin for us, so that in him we might become the righteousness of God."*

Jesus died in our place. This is how the penalty of sin was paid, how the power of death was broken, and how the victory was won. It was not by circumventing death, but by absorbing it and exhausting it. Only someone truly sinless could endure death as punishment without deserving it. And only someone truly divine could carry the full weight of humanity's guilt. Jesus was both. His death was not an accident. It was an atoning act, the decisive blow against death's reign.

Living in the light of victory

Of course, to say that death is defeated is not to say that it is gone. Christians still die. Grief still cuts deep. Funerals still happen. But we face death differently — not with despair, but with hope which is grounded in truth.

We know that death is not the end. We know that Christ has passed through it and emerged victorious. We know that because He lives, we too will live (John 14:19).

This transforms not only our understanding of eternity, but our experience of the present. The fear of death is broken. The slavery of condemnation is lifted. The bitterness of loss is softened. The sting of grief is tempered by the assurance that death will not win. And so we proclaim — in life, in ministry, in mourning, in hope: *"Thanks be to God! He gives us the victory through our Lord Jesus Christ."*(1 Corinthians 15:57)

The believer's relationship to death

Because Christ has conquered death, the believer's relationship to death is transformed. It is no longer a fearful unknown or a final defeat. Instead, it becomes — paradoxically — a moment of union with Christ and a gateway to fuller life. Still an enemy, yes, but an enemy whose power has been broken, whose sting has been removed.

Paul expresses this profound reality in Philippians 1:21-23: *"For to me, to live is Christ and to die is gain. If I am to go on living in the body, this will mean fruitful labour for me. Yet what shall I choose? I do not know! I am torn between the two: I desire to depart and be with Christ, which is better by far."*

To die is gain. Not because death itself is desirable, but because death for the Christian means departing to be with Christ. The one who defeated death now receives His people through it. Death becomes the passage, not the punishment.

2 Corinthians 5:8 echoes the same hope: *"We are confident, I say, and would prefer to be away from the body and at home with the Lord."* This language of confidence and preference would make no sense unless something radical had changed. That "something" is the cross. In Christ, the believer does not taste death as judgment. The wrath that once stood behind death has been absorbed. Now, even as we pass through death, we do so with Christ as our companion, not our judge.

This is why Paul can write in Romans 8:38–39: *"For I am convinced that neither death nor life... will be able to separate us from the love of God that is in Christ Jesus our Lord."* Death no longer separates us from God. Instead, it draws us deeper into His presence. The thing that once symbolized our banishment now marks our arrival. The wall becomes a doorway. The exile becomes a homecoming.

The church: a community of resurrection hope

In light of the cross and resurrection, the church is called to be more than just a community that preaches life — it must be a community that embodies resurrection hope in a world still ruled by the fear of death. This has always been part of the church's witness. In the early centuries of persecution, the courage of Christian martyrs stunned the Roman world. These men and women went to their deaths not with despair but with songs, prayers, and peace. Why? Because they had seen something stronger than death. They had come to know the One who had passed through the grave and risen victorious.

The church today must reclaim this witness. We do not seek death, nor do we downplay its pain. But we refuse to be enslaved by it. We comfort the grieving, bury the dead, and preach the resurrection. We resist the culture's attempts to sentimentalize or sterilize death. Instead, we name it for what it is — the last enemy — and we proclaim its defeat.

Funerals in the church should not be empty rituals. They should be bold proclamations of hope. Not cliché, not avoidance — but honest grief anchored in the gospel's victory. As Paul writes in 1 Thessalonians 4:13–14: *"Brothers and sisters, we do not want you to be uninformed about those who sleep in death, so that you do not grieve like the rest of mankind, who have no hope. For we believe that Jesus died and rose again..."*

This is the foundation of Christian mourning. We do grieve — but not as the world does. Our tears are real, but they are not hopeless. They fall with the knowledge that resurrection is coming.

This resurrection hope also fuels our courage. It empowers mission. The fear of death often paralyzes people — it keeps them from sacrificial love, from bold witness, from enduring suffering. But the one who knows that death is defeated can live with holy fearlessness. The missionary, the martyr, the suffering saint — all stand not in the absence of fear, but in the presence of victory.

As Paul says in 2 Corinthians 4:11-14: *"For we who are alive are always being given over to death for Jesus' sake... But we know that the one who raised the Lord Jesus from the dead will also raise us with Jesus."* This is the church's calling: to carry the death of Jesus in our bodies so that the life of Jesus may be revealed in the world.

How the victory of the cross shapes everyday hope

Victory over death is not just a doctrinal truth. It is a daily anchor — a foundation for how we live, suffer, endure, and prepare to die. The Christian who understands the victory of the cross sees every moment in light of eternity.

We live with courage, not anxiety

If death is defeated, then fear loses its grip. We are free to take risks for the Kingdom — to love sacrificially, to serve selflessly, to speak boldly. The worst the world can do is send us to Jesus. Our future is not fragile. It is secured in the resurrected Christ. Jesus said, *"Do not be afraid of those who kill the body but cannot kill the soul."* (Matthew 10:28). When death loses its sting, so do the threats that rely on it. This makes the Christian uniquely resilient.

We endure suffering with perspective

Suffering in this world often feels overwhelming — especially when linked to loss, illness, or grief. But the cross tells us that suffering is not the final word. The One who endured the cross now reigns in glory. And He invites us to share in both His suffering and His glory. As Paul writes: *"I consider that our present sufferings are not worth comparing with the glory that will be revealed in us."* (Romans 8:18)

This is not a call to minimize pain. It is a call to measure it against eternity. When we remember the victory of the cross, we gain strength to persevere.

We approach death with peace, not panic

Christian history is full of stories of believers who faced death with calm assurance — not because they denied its pain, but because they knew its outcome. From early martyrs to modern saints, the testimony is the same: death is not the end.

Psalm 116:15 says, *"Precious in the sight of the Lord is the death of his faithful servants."* This is not romanticism — this is divine perspective. The believer who dies in Christ is not lost. They are received. Their death is not meaningless. It is precious. This gives us peace, whether we face our own death or walk with others through theirs. We do not have to pretend or force smiles. But we do not panic. We speak truth. We offer presence. We rest in the hope that Jesus has gone before us.

We proclaim the gospel with urgency

If death is real and judgment is coming, then the message of the cross is not optional — it is essential. The victory of Christ must be proclaimed to all who are still under death's shadow. The church does not exist to offer religious comfort. It exists to announce resurrection. To speak of sin, death, judgment — and then to shout the name of Jesus, risen and reigning. Evangelism is not merely invitation. It is proclamation of victory. Paul summarizes it in 2 Corinthians 5:20: *"We are therefore Christ's ambassadors, as though God were making his appeal through us. We implore you on Christ's behalf: Be reconciled to God."* This is the appeal of the cross — be reconciled. Come out of death. Come into life. Trust the One who died and rose again.

Anticipating the final victory

Though Christ's victory is already won, we still live in the tension of the *"already and not yet."* Death is already defeated but not yet destroyed. The grave still claims bodies. Tears still fall. Sorrow still lingers. But it will not always be so.

1 Corinthians 15:51-52,54 – give us this promise: *"Listen, I tell you a mystery: We will not all sleep, but we will all be changed — in a flash, in the twinkling of an eye, at the last trumpet... Then the saying that is written will come true: 'Death has been swallowed up in victory.'"*

This is the Christian's ultimate hope. The resurrection is not just a doctrine. It is a destiny. The victory of the cross guarantees the coming of a day when death will die, once and for all. When graves will be emptied. When bodies will rise. When tears will be wiped away and we will see Him face to face. And until that day, we live in the light of what has already been accomplished.

The final destruction of death

Though death has been decisively defeated in the resurrection of Christ, the consummation of that victory lies ahead. The New Testament holds out a vision of a future day when death — not just as an experience, but as a power — will be fully and finally destroyed.

Revelation 20 depicts the final judgment. After Satan is cast into the lake of fire, John writes: *"Then death and Hades were thrown into the lake of fire. The lake of fire is the second death."* This is a stunning image: death itself is destroyed. That which ruled over all people since Adam; that which always seemed absolute and irreversible; is cast away forever. It is personified, judged, and eliminated. This is not symbolic poetry. It is theological reality. Death will not reign forever. It will die.

And then comes Revelation 21 — one of the most hopeful chapters in all of Scripture: *"He will wipe every tear from their eyes. There will be no more death or mourning or crying or pain, for the old order of things has passed away."*

This is not just comfort. It is a reordering of reality. The first creation was marred by sin and death. The new creation will be untouched by either. No funerals. No tombstones. No partings. No hospitals. No goodbyes. The Lamb who was slain will shepherd His people and they will dwell with Him in unbroken, unending life.

This is the end of the story — not darkness, but dawn. Not decay, but renewal. Not extinction, but resurrection life in a resurrected world. The Christian hope is not to escape death's grip, but to see it utterly broken. Not just for us individually, but for the universe as a whole.

Death in the plan of redemption

If death is an enemy, why does God allow it to continue? Why not eliminate it immediately after Christ's resurrection? The answer lies in the mystery of God's redemptive plan — where even His enemies are used for His purposes before they are vanquished. Death, though evil, is not sovereign. God is. And He uses even death to awaken, to humble, and to refine.

Ecclesiastes 7:2 says: *"It is better to go to a house of mourning than to go to a house of feasting, for death is the destiny of everyone; the living should take this to heart."* This is not morbid. It is wise. Death reminds us that life is fragile, time is short, and eternity is near. It disrupts our illusions of control. It punctures our pride. It calls us to number our days and seek God's wisdom (Psalm 90:12).

In this way, death, though still an enemy, becomes a messenger, a signpost pointing us back to God. It reveals the bankruptcy of sin, the limits of self-sufficiency, the need for grace. It sobers the careless, humbles the proud, and prepares the soil of the heart for the gospel. Even the fear of death, when rightly understood, can lead to life. Hebrews 2 speaks of those who were *"held in slavery by their fear of death."* But it was Christ's entry into death that broke all their chains. Fear, when met with truth, becomes a doorway to hope. And for the believer, death serves one final purpose: it is the last step into glory.

Paul writes in 2 Timothy 4:6-8, facing his own execution: *"The time for my departure is near. I have fought the good fight, I have finished the race, I have kept the faith... Now there is in store for me the crown of righteousness."* For Paul, death was not just defeat avoided — it was victory completed. Not because death had power, but because Christ did. Death was simply the final stretch of a faithful life. The last breath before glory.

Death's defeat shapes everything

To say that death has been defeated is not only to make a bold theological claim — it is to completely redefine reality. The entire shape of the Christian life is marked by this truth. Death no longer dictates our values, our fears, or our hopes.

Every time the church gathers, it sings not in denial of death, but in defiance of it. The resurrection is not just a seasonal truth for Easter — it is the permanent backdrop of our praise. The early church met on Sunday — the day Jesus rose — to clearly mark their identity as resurrection people. Their songs, prayers, and sacraments proclaimed: He is risen — and so shall we be. Every baptism is a burial and resurrection. Every Communion meal remembers death defeated. Every funeral in Christ is a loud declaration: death does not win.

Suffering finds meaning

Because of the cross, death and pain are no longer senseless. They are not good in themselves, but they can be used by God for good. Suffering becomes fellowship with Christ (Phil. 3:10). Even death itself becomes a participation in His story. This doesn't remove the agony — but it reframes it. Christians suffer not with resignation, but with resurrection in view.

Mission gains urgency

Knowing that death still claims the lost, the church must proclaim the gospel with compassion and boldness. The message of Christ crucified and risen is not a private comfort — it is a public announcement. To a world enslaved by death, we offer news of its conqueror. Evangelism is not about growing churches. It's about rescuing the dying, offering eternal life in a dying age. The victory of Christ compels us to speak.

Dying becomes witness

Perhaps nothing in Christian life is more countercultural than how believers face death. In a world that hides from mortality, the Christian faces it with open eyes and open hands.

Whether through long illness or sudden tragedy, whether in peace or pain, the dying Christian testifies: *"Jesus lives — and so shall I."* This witness, often quiet and unseen, is among the most powerful. It is not bravado. It is trust. It is the echo of Christ's own words: *"Into your hands I commit my spirit."* And it reminds the world that something stronger than death has come.

The cross: the turning point of all history

The cross is not just a doctrine to be believed. It is the turning point of all history — the moment when the tide turned, when death's dominion began to crumble, when the serpent's head was struck, when the curse was absorbed by the Lamb of God. Jesus did not go to the cross reluctantly. He went *"for the joy set before him."* (Hebrews 12:2). That joy was the joy of resurrection, of redemption, of reunion — the joy of destroying death by dying and rising to reign.

He said, *"It is finished."* And it was. The penalty of sin. The grip of death. The threat of judgment. All finished. Now, all who are in Him share in that victory. Not partially, not symbolically — but fully and eternally. *"For if we have been united with him in a death like his, we will certainly also be united with him in a resurrection like his."* (Romans 6:5). This is the promise. This is the hope. This is the gospel.

Living between the cross and the crown

We live in the time between the cross and the crown. Death's back is broken, but its shadow still falls. We still mourn. We still bury. We still ache. But not as before. Because of the cross, we live with eyes lifted. We know where history is headed. We know who holds the keys of death and Hades. We know that our Redeemer lives (Job 19:25-26) - and that in our flesh, we shall see God. So, we live and die as people of the cross and resurrection. We name death honestly. We grieve deeply. We hope defiantly. We proclaim boldly. And we wait — with certainty — for the day when the trumpet sounds, the graves break open, and death is swallowed up forever.

4. THE BELIEVER'S DEATH: PRECIOUS TO THE LORD

"Precious in the sight of the Lord is the death of his faithful servants." (Psalm 116:15) This verse is more than poetic comfort. It is a staggering revelation of divine perspective. In a world where death is feared, avoided, and often seen as failure, God calls the death of His saints *"precious."* Not pitiful. Not tragic. Precious. This invites us into a sacred paradox — one where what breaks our hearts draws also heaven's attention, where the end of a believer's earthly journey is seen not as loss, but as gain, arrival, and glory.

This chapter invites us to reconsider how we view the death of a believer. Not with shallow denial or forced optimism, but through the lens of biblical truth. The believer's death is still death — the body fails, the heart stops, the mourners weep. But it is no longer a curse. It is no longer defeat. It is now, by God's own declaration, a moment of great worth in His sight.

The Shepherd who walks with us

To understand why the believer's death is precious, we must begin with the presence of the Lord in death. The God who numbers our days (Psalm 139:16) is not a distant observer when those days come to an end. He is near. Psalm 23, beloved across the centuries, offers this promise: *"Even though I walk through the valley of the shadow of death, I will fear no evil, for you are with me; your rod and your staff, they comfort me."*

Notice the shift in address. Earlier in the psalm, David refers to God in the third person: *"He makes me lie down... He leads me..."* But here, in the shadow of death, David now speaks directly: *"You are with me."* The language becomes personal, intimate, immediate. In life's darkest moment, God draws closest. Again, this is not poetic imagination - it is theological truth. The believer does not die alone. Even if no family is present. Even if the room is silent. Even if death comes suddenly. The Good Shepherd is there.

The One who laid down His life for the sheep now walks with them through their own final valley — not as a guide from a distance, but as a faithful Companion. There is no valley He hasn't walked Himself. Jesus tasted death fully — not to spare us from dying, but to transform what death would mean. Now, the shadow may fall, but the light is near. The Shepherd remains.

The departure that is gain

The Apostle Paul faced death often - through persecution, in prison, and ultimately in martyrdom. Yet he could write with startling clarity: *"For to me, to live is Christ and to die is gain."* (Philippians 1:21).

This is not stoicism. It is not denial. Paul is not dismissing the pain or fear that may accompany death. Instead, he is reframing its meaning in light of Christ.

To live is Christ — every breath, every step, every moment of obedience is marked by union with Jesus. But to die? That's more of Christ, not less. Not separation, but arrival. Not loss, but gain. He continues: *"I desire to depart and be with Christ, which is better by far."* (Philippians 1:23)

Death for the believer is not an end. It is departure — a word that evokes concepts like setting sail, breaking camp, or going home. It is a transition, not a termination. The soul leaves behind the broken body, the cursed world, the groaning creation — and enters into the unfiltered presence of Christ.

That is the gain. Not floating in a misty realm. Not unconscious sleep. But being with Christ — seeing the face we've trusted, hearing the voice we've followed, entering the joy we've longed for all these years.

This is why Paul does not romanticize death, but neither does he dread it. For the believer, death has become a homecoming. The One who died for us now receives us into His presence. There is no gap. No waiting room. Just Christ.

Conscious communion with Christ

Some have suggested that after death, the soul enters a kind of sleep until the resurrection. But Scripture consistently presents a different picture — one of immediate, conscious fellowship with the Lord.

When Jesus hung on the cross, one of the criminals beside Him cried out for mercy. Jesus responded: *"Truly I tell you, today you will be with me in paradise."* (Luke 23:43). Not someday. Not after a long wait. Today. That very day, the thief — once condemned, now redeemed — would be with Jesus, in paradise. This is not soul sleep. It is conscious communion. The thief's final breath became his first moment in glory.

Paul reaffirms this in 2 Corinthians 5: *"We are confident, I say, and would prefer to be away from the body and at home with the Lord."* To be absent from the body is not to be unconscious, but to be present with the Lord. There is no delay. No limbo. The body sleeps in the grave, awaiting resurrection. But the soul, cleansed by grace, goes immediately to Christ.

This truth has comforted believers for centuries. The dying are not slipping into a silent void. They are being welcomed into the presence of the One they have loved from afar.

Angels watching, angels carrying

Jesus' parable of the rich man and Lazarus (Luke 16) gives a striking detail: *"The time came when the beggar died and the angels carried him to Abraham's side."* Though a parable, the imagery reflects a consistent biblical theme: angels are sent by God to minister to His people, especially in critical moments. Hebrews calls them *"ministering spirits sent to serve those who will inherit salvation."* (1:14). Could any moment of need be greater than our final breath?

Though unseen, we can imagine angels gathering in the room, not to remove the soul, but to escort it home. Not as grim reapers, but as joyful bearers of glory.

Death for the believer is not a fall into the abyss. It is a lifting up — a receiving, a carrying, a welcoming. The unseen world comes alive in that moment, not to threaten, but to celebrate. Heaven moves to receive one of its own.

The final testimony of a faithful life

The believer's death, far from being a footnote, becomes the final testimony of a faithful life. It is not the erasure of witness, but its final punctuation mark. Hebrews 11, the great *'hall of faith,'* ends with a declaration: *"These were all commended for their faith… they were still living by faith when they died."*

Death does not interrupt faith. It completes it. It fulfils what faith longed for. For all their days, these saints believed without seeing. At death, faith became sight. Their witness did not end; it was sealed in glory.

This is why the Psalmist can say with confidence, *"Precious in the sight of the Lord is the death of his faithful servants."* God is not indifferent. He is watching. He is near. He is receiving. We mourn, but not as those without hope. We weep, but not in despair. For the believer, death is the doorway to reward, to rest, to reunion — and to Christ Himself.

"Then I heard a voice from heaven say, 'Write this: Blessed are the dead who die in the Lord from now on.' 'Yes,' says the Spirit, 'they will rest from their labour, for their deeds will follow them.'" (Revelation 14:13)

These words echo from heaven to earth, proclaiming a truth we would never dare assume apart from divine revelation: Blessed are the dead who die in the Lord. Not pitied. Not cursed. Blessed.

The Christian vision of death is not one of mere escape or resignation. It is rest, reward, and remembrance. The rest is from earthly toil and sorrow, the reward is Christ Himself, and the remembrance is not forgotten deeds, but eternal impact. What a contrast to the world's view of death as extinguishing all meaning. For those in Christ, death magnifies meaning.

The end of labour, not life

The Revelation passage proclaims, *"They will rest from their labour."* Death for the believer is not an erasure of personhood or purpose. It is the cessation of wearying toil. This is not sleep in the sense of unconsciousness, but Sabbath — a divine pause, a holy cessation of burdens.

Throughout Scripture, rest is a rich and layered promise. In Hebrews 4, we are told: *"There remains, then, a Sabbath-rest for the people of God; for anyone who enters God's rest also rests from their works, just as God did from his."*

This *"Sabbath-rest"* is both now and not yet — we taste it now in worship and obedience, but we enter it fully at death, where striving ceases, and God's peace fully envelops the soul. For the believer, death is not a shutdown. It is a laying down — of burdens, temptations, griefs, fears, disappointment, pain and sorrow. It is the start of rest more than the end of life.

Our culture prizes productivity, glorifies hustle, and avoids stillness. But in the kingdom of God, rest is holy. And the death of the believer — marked not by frantic grasping, but peaceful surrender — becomes the final and fullest entry into God's rest.

The reward of the faithful

"They will rest from their labour, for their deeds will follow them." This promise is subtle but profound. Our deeds do not save us — only Christ does that. But our works, born of faith, are not forgotten. They follow us. Not to haunt us, but to bear witness. Not to condemn, but to confirm.

Scripture consistently affirms that there will be reward for the faithful. Jesus said in Matthew 10: *"If anyone gives even a cup of cold water to one of these little ones who is my disciple... that person will certainly not lose their reward."* Hebrews 6 reminds us: *"God is not unjust; he will not forget your work and the love you have shown him as you have helped his people."* Even the smallest act of faith, kindness, or service — done in Christ — echoes in eternity.

The believer's death does not erase their story; It brings it into eternal remembrance. Their deeds follow them, not to define them, but to decorate the grace of God already theirs. What comfort this brings! The sacrifices no one saw. The prayers no one heard. The faithfulness no one celebrated. God saw. God heard. God remembers. Death does not end that. It unveils it.

Mourning with hope

Of course, death still wounds us. Even for the believer, there is great pain in parting. Jesus Himself wept at the tomb of Lazarus, though He knew resurrection was moments away. His tears remind us that grief is not a lack of faith — it is love in sorrow. But the death of a believer brings a unique kind of grief — one which is infused with hope.

"Brothers and sisters, we do not want you to be uninformed about those who sleep in death, so that you do not grieve like the rest of mankind, who have no hope." (1 Thessalonians 4:13) Notice Paul does not say we do not grieve. We do. Deeply. But not like the rest of the world. We grieve with hope, with assurance, with the promise that this separation is temporary. The grave does not speak the final word. Christ does. Hope does not cancel sorrow. It transforms it.

Christian grief is a blend of ache and anticipation, pain and praise, tears and trust. We bury our loved ones in the soil of resurrection. We lay them down, but not in despair. We sow them like seeds, awaiting the harvest of new creation.

Christian funerals should look different

Because of all this, the way we mark the death of believers must be different. Not sterile rituals or hollow celebration. Not denial or sentimentality. But hopeful realism, which is marked by worship, gratitude, and testimony. The early church treated the death of believers not as loss, but as promotion. They called it *"a falling asleep,"* not because they denied its pain, but because they believed in a coming awakening.

Funerals were often held in catacombs — not just tombs, but places of hope, etched with biblical inscriptions like *"She lives in Christ"* or *"He awaits the resurrection."*

We should not grieve like the world, nor should we celebrate like we don't grieve. A Christian funeral is a declaration of the gospel: that Christ is risen, that death is defeated, and that our brother or sister is more alive now than they have ever been. Songs should rise. Scriptures should ring. The gospel should be preached. Why? Because the believer's death is precious in God's sight, and the gathering of saints in mourning becomes a testimony to the resurrection life we share.

The death of saints as a witness

The death of a believer often speaks louder than their life. There is something deeply moving — even compelling — about a saint who faces death with peace, confidence, and worship. Think of Stephen in Acts 7. As he was stoned for his faith, his face shone like an angel. He saw heaven opened and Jesus standing at the right hand of God. As he died, he prayed for his killers, echoing his Saviour. His death was not just tragic. It was a powerful witness. And from that moment, the gospel surged forward.

Or consider Paul, facing execution, writing in 1 Timothy 4:7: *"I have fought the good fight, I have finished the race, I have kept the faith. Now there is in store for me the crown of righteousness, which the Lord, the righteous Judge, will award to me on that day."*

What assurance. What clarity. What a legacy. The world watches how we live. But it also watches how we die. A believer who dies clinging to Christ becomes a final sermon, a final song, a final act of faith. Their life on earth ends, but their testimony does not.

Death as a defeated enemy

Even as we call death precious for the believer, we must always remember death is still an enemy. Paul calls it *"the last enemy to be destroyed."* (1 Corinthians 15:26). It is not our friend. It is not natural. It is the result of sin and the fracture of creation.

But it is an enemy defeated in Christ. On the cross, Jesus bore the full curse of death. In the tomb, He lay under its weight. But on the third day, He rose — not just for Himself, but for us. His resurrection is the guarantee of ours. The first fruits. The down payment. The preview.

So even as we acknowledge the pain of death, we proclaim its doom. It may strike, but it cannot destroy. It may wound, but it cannot win. The believer dies, but they do not perish. They pass through death into life.

And one day, that enemy will be fully destroyed. The trumpet will sound. The dead will be raised. Mortality will be swallowed up by immortality. And then we will say: *"Where, O death, is your victory? Where, O death, is your sting?"* (1 Corinthians 15:55). Until that day, we live in the tension of grief and glory, sorrow and song, cross and crown.

So, we must remember that Paul's words in Philippians 1:23 are not poetic escapism or theological speculation. They are a profound declaration of hope. *"I desire to depart and be with Christ, which is better by far."* For the apostle, death was not something to fear — it was a doorway into a deeper union with Christ. To depart from this life was, in his own words, *"better by far."* But why? What lies beyond the grave for the believer that makes death not a tragedy, but a treasure? Let us explore the mystery and majesty of what awaits those who die in the Lord — not merely in imagination, but as revealed in Scripture.

With Christ immediately

Paul is unequivocal: to die is to be with Christ. Not to enter soul-sleep or a holding cell of the spirit, but to be present with the Lord. *"We are confident, I say, and would prefer to be away from the body and at home with the Lord."* (2 Corinthians 5:8).

At the moment of death, the believer goes home — not in a vague spiritual sense, but in a deeply personal, relational way. Home is where Christ is. And Christ is not far off. He is near, waiting to receive His own.

Don't forget the assurance of Jesus to the thief on the cross: *"Truly I tell you, today you will be with me in paradise."* (Luke 23:43). Not tomorrow. Not someday. Today. This is the intermediate state — the period between death and resurrection. While the body rests in the earth, the soul is consciously present with Christ. It is paradise, yes. But it is not yet the final chapter. For even greater glory awaits.

Resurrection: the Christian's ultimate hope

Although the soul's immediate presence with Christ is glorious, the Bible teaches that the fullness of salvation includes the resurrection of the body. *"For the Lord himself will come down from heaven, with a loud command... and the dead in Christ will rise first."* (1 Thessalonians 4:16). And in 1 Corinthians 15:52, *"The trumpet will sound, the dead will be raised imperishable, and we will be changed."*

This is not metaphor. It is material, bodily resurrection. The same Jesus who walked out of the tomb in a glorified body will raise His people with new, incorruptible bodies — physical, yet perfected. Christian hope is not about escaping the body; it's about redeeming it. Salvation is not a spiritual abstraction; it is holistic. God made all of us - body and soul - and He intends to save both.

That's why the grave is not our final home. The body may return to dust, but it is not discarded. It is sown in weakness, raised in power. The Christian dead lie in hope, awaiting the call of their Shepherd, who will one day say again, *"Come forth."*

The new heavens and new earth

Where will we dwell after the resurrection? Not in some abstract heavenly realm, but in a renewed creation — the New Heavens and the New Earth. *"Then I saw 'a new heaven and a new earth,' for the first heaven and the first earth had passed away... And I heard a loud voice from the throne saying, 'Look! God's dwelling place is now among the people, and he will dwell with them. They will be his people, and God himself will be with them and be their God."*

"He will wipe every tear from their eyes. There will be no more death or mourning or crying or pain, for the old order of things has passed away."' (Revelation 21:1-4).

This is the final destination. Not a disembodied eternity in the clouds, but a renewed cosmos in which righteousness dwells. The New Jerusalem is not an escape from earth but a marriage of heaven and earth. It is here that death is finally, fully undone. *"The last enemy to be destroyed is death."* (1 Corinthians 15:26).

And destroyed it shall be. There will come a day when death will die. No more coffins. No more farewells. No more digging graves. No more crematoriums. The one who conquered death will erase it from His creation. That is the end of the story — or rather, the beginning of the endless joy.

A better country

The letter to the Hebrews speaks of those who lived by faith and died in faith, never receiving the fullness of God's promise on earth: *"They admitted that they were foreigners and strangers on earth… They were longing for a better country — a heavenly one. Therefore, God is not ashamed to be called their God, for he has prepared a city for them."* (Hebrews 11:13-16).

Here is a glimpse into the heart of God. The Lord delights in those who long for the life to come — not in despair or denial, but in holy expectation. To die in Christ is to step into the better country that God Himself has prepared. When a believer dies, they do not vanish into mystery. They enter the reality that faith has long anticipated.

Death and the communion of saints

There is one more truth to lift our eyes beyond the grave — the fellowship of God's people across time and space. The church is not divided by death. We speak of the church militant (those still on earth) and the church triumphant (those who have died in Christ). But there is one church, one body, one Bride of Christ. The saints who have gone before us are not gone.

They are ahead. Not asleep, but alive in the presence of God, worshipping, waiting, and watching. Hebrews 12:1 tells us, *"Therefore, since we are surrounded by such a great cloud of witnesses…"* Again, this is not just poetic license — it is a glimpse of eternal reality. The believer who dies is not lost to us. They are joined to that great cloud, cheering us on as we run the race set before us.

Precious in His sight

So why does Scripture say that the death of his faithful servants is precious to the Lord (Psalm 116:15)? Because God delights to welcome His children home. Because their suffering is over. Because they are now where they were always meant to be — with Him.

It does not mean death is easy. It does not mean we don't grieve. But we do not grieve as those without hope. The tears are real — but so is the triumph. The death of a believer is precious because it marks the moment when faith becomes sight, when worship becomes face-to-face, when striving becomes rest, and when longing is finally fulfilled.

Living in light of dying well

If the believer's death is precious, how then should we live? We should live as those who are prepared to die, whenever that may come – not with dread, but with peace. We should labour in the kingdom with our eyes fixed on eternity. We should mourn differently, grieve hopefully, and die trusting Jesus.

We should treasure what God treasures. We should honour the memory of faithful saints. We should remind each other — often — that the best is yet to come. Most of all, we should make it our aim, like Paul, to please the Lord — whether by life or by death — knowing that for those in Christ, death has lost its sting.

5. TO DIE IS GAIN: THE INTERMEDIATE STATE

The Christian confession that *"to die is gain"* stands in sharp contrast to the instinctive human dread of death. For many, death is the end of all that is known and loved, a void into which people disappear with no assurance of what lies beyond. But for the believer in Jesus Christ, death is not the terminus of existence but the doorway to a fuller communion with God.

This conviction is rooted in Scripture's teaching about what theologians call the intermediate state — the conscious condition of the soul between the moment of physical death and the resurrection of the body at Christ's return. This chapter explores the biblical foundation and the pastoral implications of this profound truth.

"To die is gain" – The Apostle Paul's hope

Paul's letter to the Philippians contains one of the most striking declarations in all of Scripture about the believer's attitude toward death: *"For to me, to live is Christ and to die is gain… I desire to depart and be with Christ, which is better by far."* (1:21, 23).

Paul writes from a Roman prison, uncertain whether he will be released or executed. And yet, in this moment of mortal threat, his confidence in Christ overflows. He does not merely tolerate the idea of death; he speaks of it as a gain — a better state. Why? Because to die is to depart and be with Christ.

The verb *"depart"* evokes imagery of setting sail, breaking camp, or being released from bondage. It speaks not of annihilation but of transition. And what lies on the other side of that departure? Being *"with Christ."* This phrase alone defines the intermediate state for Paul. The believer's soul, upon death, is not lost in unconsciousness or consigned to some shadowy limbo. Rather, it enters into the very presence of the Lord. This is what makes death a gain: not freedom from pain, not escape from a broken world, but communion with the risen Christ.

This is not an isolated statement from Paul. His confidence in the intermediate state appears again in his second letter to the Corinthians: *"We are confident, I say, and would prefer to be away from the body and at home with the Lord."* (2 Corinthians 5:8). Here, Paul reinforces the idea of a conscious existence after death.

The believer, upon being *"away from the body"* — that is, dead in the physical sense - is *"at home with the Lord."* There is no gap, no soul-sleep, no unconscious interval. The death of the believer is immediately followed by life in God's presence.

What is the intermediate state?

The term *"intermediate state"* refers to the temporary condition of believers between their physical death and their future bodily resurrection at the return of Christ. Scripture teaches that the final destiny of God's people is not a disembodied spiritual existence but the resurrection of the body and life in the new heavens and new earth (Revelation 21-22; 1 Corinthians 15).

However, the period between death and resurrection is not one of nonexistence or dormancy. Rather, believers live in conscious fellowship with God in a true spiritual state, awaiting the full redemption of their personal bodies. Theologians throughout church history have affirmed this doctrine.

The Westminster Confession of Faith (1646) puts it this way:

"The bodies of men, after death, return to dust... but their souls... do immediately return to God... The souls of the righteous... are received into the highest heavens, where they behold the face of God in light and glory, waiting for the full redemption of their bodies."

While the term intermediate state is not found in Scripture, the concept is clearly present. It helps us distinguish between the already-realised blessing of being with Christ and the not-yet-fulfilled hope of bodily resurrection. In this way, it guards against both overstatement (as though heaven is the final destination) and understatement (as though nothing happens after death until the end).

Jesus and the thief on the cross

Perhaps the clearest affirmation of the intermediate state comes from Jesus Himself in Luke 23:42-43. As He hangs dying on the cross, one of the criminals crucified beside Him turns to him and says: *"Jesus, remember me when you come into your kingdom."* Jesus answered him, *"Truly I tell you, today you will be with me in paradise."*

This simple exchange dismantles the notion that the dead enter an unconscious sleep. Jesus does not say, *"One day, after the resurrection, you will be with me,"* or *"After a long waiting period, we'll see each other again."* He says, *"Today."* That very day, both Jesus and the penitent thief would die physically — but their souls would continue to exist, united in a place Jesus calls *"paradise."* The word paradise here evokes the garden imagery of Eden restored. It is not yet the new creation in its fullness, but it is a place of peace, rest, and divine presence.

More importantly, Jesus' promise is deeply personal: *"You will be with me."* Again, the defining feature of the intermediate state is not a place, but a Person. The reward of faith is to be where Jesus is.

Conscious fellowship, not soul sleep

Some traditions have taught that after death, the soul enters a state of unconscious rest, often called *"soul sleep,"* until the resurrection. While well-intentioned, perhaps seeking to protect the finality of resurrection, this view falls short of the biblical witness.

As we've seen, Paul speaks of death as a conscious homecoming. Jesus promises immediate paradise. In Revelation 6, the souls of martyrs cry out from beneath the altar, asking how long it will be until justice is done. (Revelation 6:9-10)

These souls are not asleep — they are awake, aware, speaking, and waiting. In Hebrews 12:23, the author refers to *"the spirits of the righteous made perfect"* who dwell in the heavenly Jerusalem. The imagery is vivid, personal, and conscious.

Moreover, the idea of *"sleep"* in Scripture is a metaphor for death — particularly from the perspective of the living. When Jesus says of Lazarus, *"Our friend Lazarus has fallen asleep,"* and then clarifies, *"Lazarus is dead,"* He affirms that sleep is a figure of speech, not a literal condition (John 11:11-14). Similarly, when Paul refers to believers who have *"fallen asleep,"* he uses common ancient language for those who have really died, not a technical doctrine of unconsciousness.

The soul's longing for its home

The intermediate state is not the final hope of the Christian — that belongs to the bodily resurrection and the renewal of all things — but it is a precious promise, nonetheless. It assures believers that the moment their earthly life ends, they are not lost, alone, or unconscious. They are at home, with Christ.

Paul's confidence in this truth sustained him in suffering and empowered him in mission. He could face death with courage because he knew it would usher him into Christ's presence. He could delay that joy for the sake of fruitful labour on earth, but he viewed his death not as a tragedy to be avoided at all costs, but as a reunion to be anticipated.

For many Christians today — especially those nearing death or grieving the loss of a loved one — this truth offers comfort beyond words. It means that those who die in Christ are not gone; they are with Him. It means that our hope does not rest in a distant future but in a present promise. And it means that even as we wait for the resurrection, we can say with full assurance: *"To die is gain."*

While the promise of being *"with Christ"* at death offers profound comfort, there is more to say about the intermediate state. This state is neither our final destination nor a form of suspended animation. It is a conscious, personal, and temporary condition of blessedness for the believer between physical death and bodily resurrection. Scripture affirms both the continuity of personal identity after death and the incompleteness of our redemptive journey until the resurrection.

Continuity of personal identity

One of the great comforts found in the teaching about the intermediate state is the continuity of personal identity. The believer who dies remains truly themselves in the presence of Christ. Death does not erase who we are; it relocates us. Paul expresses this continuity clearly in 2 Corinthians 5:8: *"We are confident, I say, and would prefer to be away from the body and at home with the Lord."* The *"we"* that departs the body is the same *"we"* that is at home with Christ. There is no loss of personhood or dissolution of the self. Rather, the soul — the inner, conscious reality of the believer — continues in fellowship with Christ, awaiting the rejoining with the body at the resurrection.

This truth is also implicit in Jesus' words to the thief on the cross in Luke 23:43: *"Truly I tell you, today you will be with me in paradise."* The thief would not become a vague soul-essence or lose his personal identity. He, the same man crucified beside Jesus, would enter paradise in communion with the Saviour. He would still be *"him,"* known and loved by the Lord.

This continuity affirms our God-given identity and personality. Our memories, our love for Christ, our yearning for redemption — these do not perish with the body. They are carried forward, purified by grace, into the presence of God. What a comfort to know that we remain fully ourselves — only now freed from sin, sorrow, and suffering.

Incomplete but safe: waiting for the resurrection

However, while the believer is truly *"with the Lord"* after death, this intermediate state is not the final stage of salvation. It is intermediate — a temporary condition between bodily death and the complete resurrection of the body at Christ's return. Paul underscores this in Romans 8:23 when he writes, *"we ourselves, who have the first fruits of the Spirit, groan inwardly as we wait eagerly for our adoption to sonship, the redemption of our bodies."* The full redemption includes not only our souls, but our bodies. Until that day, the saints in heaven wait — secure, joyful, but not yet glorified in body.

This distinction prevents us from collapsing the intermediate state with the eternal state. Heaven, as commonly spoken of, is often imagined as the believer's final home. But biblically speaking, the final destination is not a disembodied heaven but the new heavens and new earth in resurrected, glorified bodies (Revelation 21:1-5). The intermediate state is glorious, but it is not yet complete.

The souls of believers, though consciously and joyfully In Christ's presence, are awaiting something. Revelation 6:9-11 presents a striking image of the martyrs crying out under the altar, *"How long, Sovereign Lord, holy and true, until you judge the inhabitants of the earth and avenge our blood?"* These saints are not asleep; they are speaking, reasoning, and longing for the fulfilment of justice and resurrection. They are at peace — and yet they await a future fulfilment.

This period of waiting is not anxious or uncertain. It is marked by peace, security, and the presence of Christ. But it is waiting, nonetheless. Even in glory, the saints will look forward to resurrection day, when Christ will reunite soul and body in perfect glorification and usher in the eternal kingdom.

What the intermediate state is <u>not</u>

Several misunderstandings about the intermediate state have persisted through the centuries, sometimes distorting biblical hope. One such error is the notion of soul sleep, which we will address more fully in the next chapter. Briefly, this is the idea that the soul becomes unconscious or inactive at death, only to be awakened at the resurrection.

This view collapses the clear biblical testimony of conscious fellowship with Christ after death, which we have already seen in Paul's confident longing to be *"with Christ"* and Jesus' promise to the thief.

Another common misunderstanding is that believers become angels after death. This idea, while popular in culture and sentimental expressions, is not biblically grounded. Humans and angels are distinct creations.

Believers who die do not grow a set of wings or become heavenly messengers. They remain human beings — glorified in soul, awaiting bodily resurrection. The intermediate state does not erase our humanity; it purifies and preserves it.

A third error is to speak of the intermediate state as our *"final resting place."* Though this phrase is common on tombstones, it obscures the dynamic biblical vision of resurrection and renewal. For believers, death is not the end — not even temporarily. The body rests, but the soul rejoices in the presence of Christ. And even the body's rest is not final. A trumpet will sound, the dead will be raised, and our perishable bodies will be clothed with the imperishable (1 Corinthians 15:51-54). The grave is not the end. The last word belongs to Christ, the resurrection and the life.

How the intermediate state shapes Christian living

Why does the doctrine of the intermediate state matter for our lives today? It matters because it anchors our hope in the presence of Christ. We do not face death with vague wishfulness or fearful speculation. We face it with confidence rooted in the promises of Scripture: *"to be away from the body is to be at home with the Lord."* (2 Corinthians 5:8). This truth offers profound comfort to believers — not only at the hour of death, but throughout all of life's trials.

The intermediate state reminds us that death does not sever us from Christ; it ushers us more fully into His presence. This changes how we view suffering, aging, and the decline of our earthly bodies. We do not fear death as the world does. We may grieve the losses it brings, but we do not grieve as those without hope (1 Thessalonians 4:13). Our hope is sure: death means being with Christ — conscious, loved, secure. This truth also shapes how we walk through the death of fellow believers. When a loved one dies in Christ, we know they are not lost or gone. They are with the Lord — more alive than ever. They are free from pain, sin, and sorrow. They are part of the *"great cloud of witnesses"* (Hebrews 12:1), cheering us on as we run the race. This comforts us in grief and inspires us in perseverance.

Finally, the intermediate state fuels our longing for the return of Christ. Knowing that our departed loved ones are with Christ gives us peace. Knowing that their resurrection is still to come keeps us yearning for the day when all things will be made new. The intermediate state is glorious, but it is not the end. We await the day when death is swallowed up forever and all creation is redeemed.

A glimpse, not a blueprint

Scripture only gives us glimpses of the intermediate state, not exhaustive descriptions. We see enough to be confident, but not so much as to be distracted. The emphasis is always on being with Christ — not on the mechanics or the scenery of the afterlife. Paul doesn't describe the architecture of paradise; he describes his deep desire to depart and be with Christ, which he just calls *"better by far"* (Philippians 1:23).

Jesus doesn't map out the afterlife for the thief on the cross; He simply says, *"Today you will be with me."* This Christ-centred focus is vital. The goal of the intermediate state is not rest or reward, but relationship. It is not about floating in bliss but fellowshipping with Jesus. The intermediate state is not our final destination — it is our safe lodging on the journey toward full redemption. And at the centre of it all is the presence of Christ.

Though the intermediate state is not the final chapter in the believer's story, it is a profoundly hopeful one. It affirms that death, while still an enemy, no longer has dominion over those who are in Christ. The moment the Christian dies, they are ushered into the conscious presence of their Lord—not as vague spirits drifting in limbo, but as real persons, known and held in the embrace of divine glory.

The unredeemed: a sobering contrast

While Scripture offers rich encouragement to those who die in the Lord, it does not paint the same picture for those outside of Christ. Jesus' story of the rich man and Lazarus (Luke 16:19–31) portrays not only a conscious awareness in the afterlife but a dramatic division between the righteous and the unrighteous.

Lazarus, the poor man, is comforted at Abraham's side, while the rich man suffers. The parable is not merely about economic disparity or lack of compassion—it is a window into the reality of life after death and the stark contrast in destinies. The rich man's request for water and a warning to his brothers makes it clear: there is no opportunity for repentance after death. The intermediate state for the unredeemed is not a place of soul sleep or second chances—it is a place of conscious separation from the presence of God, a foretaste of the final judgment to come. This sobering truth heightens the urgency of the gospel.

As Paul reminds the Corinthians, *"Now is the time of God's favour, now is the day of salvation."* (2 Corinthians 6:2). The doctrine of the intermediate state does not allow for neutral ground. There is no purgatory, no spiritual limbo in which souls might evolve or earn their way into paradise. The line is drawn at death: either *"to be with Christ"* (Philippians 1:23) or to be apart from Him. This is not a cause for fear in the believer but a call to loving urgency for the world.

The witness of the martyrs

Throughout church history, those who have faced death for the sake of Christ have found courage and peace in the assurance of the intermediate state. The early church fathers often spoke of *"falling asleep in the Lord"* as a beautiful transition into a nearer communion with God. The martyr Stephen, as he was being stoned, cried out, *"Lord Jesus, receive my spirit"* (Acts 7:59). That cry was not metaphor—it was the confident trust of a man who knew that his body would fall, but his soul would rise into the arms of Christ.

This same assurance sustained persecuted believers throughout the centuries. From the Roman coliseums to the missionary fields of the modern world, Christians have faced death not as a bleak wall but as a doorway. Paul's words in Philippians 1:21-24 ring out as a defiant hope: *"To live is Christ and to die is gain... I desire to depart and be with Christ, which is better by far."* This is not death-denial, but death-redeemed. It is the triumph of faith over fear, of hope over finality.

Even in the final words of dying saints, we hear echoes of this truth. John Wesley reportedly said with his last breath, *"The best of all is, God is with us."* D.L. Moody declared on his deathbed, *"Earth recedes, heaven opens before me."* These are not sentimental illusions—they are expressions of deep theological conviction rooted in Scripture. Death was not a descent into shadow, but a movement into radiant glory.

Shaping our present hope

The doctrine of the intermediate state is not just for the dying—it is for the living. It reshapes how we view suffering, grief, and endurance. When Paul says in 2 Corinthians 5:8, *"We are confident ... and would prefer to be away from the body and at home with the Lord,"* he is not promoting escapism. He is giving voice to a yearning that coexists with obedience. Until Christ returns, we live in the tension of presence and promise. But that tension is held in hope.

This hope allows us to grieve deeply without despair. It gives comfort to those who sit beside hospital beds and gravesides. When we say goodbye to a believing loved one, we do not say it into a void—we say it into the arms of Christ, trusting that they are now with Him. We do not imagine them floating in some abstract heavenly ether, but truly alive, aware, and joyfully safe.

Furthermore, this hope empowers mission. If death truly is gain for the believer, then life must be lived for Christ with urgency and passion. Paul, even as he longed to depart, chose to remain *"for your progress and joy in the faith"* (Philippians 1:25). The promise of heaven does not lull the church into passivity—it awakens her to the worth of every soul, the power of every moment, and the glory of her calling.

Bridging the now and the not yet

There is a profound mystery in the intermediate state. We cannot fully comprehend what it means to be *"away from the body and at home with the Lord,"* because we have never experienced this disembodied existence.

And yet the Scriptures are very clear that such a state is real, conscious, and joy-filled. It is not the end of the story, but it is a glorious chapter in the journey of redemption.

We therefore must resist the temptation to reduce heaven to our imaginations or to project onto it all our own unfulfilled earthly desires. The joy of being with Christ is not primarily about celestial scenery or reunion with loved ones—it is about Him. The true longing of the Christian heart is not merely for relief or restoration, but for the presence of the Redeemer.

As believers, we wait eagerly not just for the moment of departure but for the great day of resurrection. Let me say it again, the intermediate state is not our final destination. The Christian hope is not to be a spirit in heaven forever—it is to be raised in glory with a new body, to reign with Christ in the new creation, when death shall be no more.

But until that day, we take heart. Because to die is gain. To die is not to lose ourselves but to find ourselves more fully. To die in Christ is not to end, but to begin anew. As Paul wrote, *"I desire to depart and be with Christ, which is better by far."* Better not because of escape, but because of presence—presence with the One who loved us and gave Himself for us.

This is the hope that anchors our souls in the storm. This is the comfort that steadies our hearts when the shadows fall. And this is the truth that sends us into the world with urgency and joy.

For to live is Christ ... and to die is gain.

6. THE METAPHOR OF 'SLEEP'

In the Bible, the metaphor of sleep is frequently used to describe death, especially the death of believers. The expression is both tender and instructive. Sleep is a temporary state; it implies rest, peace, and the expectation of waking.

When Scripture says that someone has *"fallen asleep,"* it is not denying the reality of death—it is reshaping the way we see it through the lens of divine hope. Understanding this metaphor rightly is essential for a biblical theology of death.

The language of sleep in the Old Testament

The metaphor of sleep to describe death is already present in the Old Testament. In 1 Kings 2:10, we read, *"Then David rested with his ancestors and was buried in the City of David."*

Similar expressions—*"slept with his fathers," "lay down,"* or *"rested"*—are common in the descriptions of kings and patriarchs (cf. 1 Kings 11:43; 14:31). These are more than euphemisms; they reflect a worldview in which death is not annihilation, but transition.

Even though the Old Testament does not reveal the afterlife with the clarity of the New Testament, it consistently portrays death as a kind of sleep. Job, amid his intense suffering, laments that he cannot simply *"lie down in death"* and find rest (Job 3:11, 13). Psalm 13:3 pleads, *"Give light to my eyes, or I will sleep in death."* Here, sleep and death are linked, not to deny death's power, but to express it in familiar and humane terms.

This use of sleep language serves to soften the harshness of death while affirming its reality. In Israel's developing theology, death was not yet fully unveiled, but even then, it was not framed as eternal oblivion. The faithful believed in a future hope, even if they could not articulate it fully at that time. As the redemptive story unfolds, the metaphor of sleep gains depth and richness, especially in the teaching of Jesus and the apostolic witness.

Jesus and the metaphor of sleep

Jesus employs the metaphor of sleep with deliberate clarity and purpose. In John 11, when Lazarus dies, Jesus tells His disciples, *"Our friend Lazarus has fallen asleep; but I am going there to wake him up."* (John 11:11). The disciples misunderstand and assume He is referring to natural sleep. Jesus then clarifies, *"Lazarus is dead"* (v.14). This moment is deeply instructive: Jesus equates death with sleep not to confuse but to reveal a profound truth—death is not final for those whom He will awaken.

This metaphor is more than poetic—it is theological. When Jesus speaks of death as sleep, He is asserting His authority over it. Just as He wakes people from physical sleep, He can summon them from the sleep of death. His command, *"Lazarus, come out!"* (John 11:43), was not only a miracle but a signpost toward the resurrection. Death, for the believer, is no more permanent than sleep when Christ is the One who calls.

The raising of Jairus's daughter further illustrates this. When Jesus arrives, the mourners are wailing, but He says, *"The child is not dead but asleep"* (Mark 5:39). The crowd laughs, thinking He is in denial. But Jesus is not being sentimental. He is speaking from the vantage point of divine power. He takes her hand and says, *"Little girl, I say to you, get up!"* (v.41). And she does.

In both cases, Jesus reframes death. The metaphor of sleep is not a denial of physical death—it is a declaration of His lordship over it. For those who belong to Him, death is a temporary condition, not a permanent fate. It is a sleep from which they will surely awaken.

Paul and the theology of sleep

The Apostle Paul embraces the metaphor of sleep with particular enthusiasm, especially when writing to the Thessalonians. In 1 Thessalonians 4:13–14, he writes: *"Brothers and sisters, we do not want you to be uninformed about those who sleep in death, so that you do not grieve like the rest of mankind, who have no hope. For we believe that Jesus died and rose again, and so we believe that God will bring with Jesus those who have fallen asleep in him."*

Here, sleep is clearly synonymous with death—but it is seen through the lens of resurrection. Paul does not minimize grief but insists that Christian grief is different. It is laced with hope, because those who have *"fallen asleep in Him"* will rise again.

Later in the same chapter, Paul describes the return of Christ and says, *"The dead in Christ will rise first"* (v.16). The implication is unmistakable: the dead are not unconscious forever. They are sleeping, awaiting the trumpet call of God. Death is sleep precisely because it ends in awakening.

In 1 Corinthians 15, Paul continues this motif, saying that Christ *"appeared to more than five hundred of the brothers and sisters at the same time, most of whom are still living, though some have fallen asleep"* (v.6). He speaks of the resurrection as the moment when *"the perishable must clothe itself with the imperishable"* (v.53), reinforcing that death is a temporary condition for the believer.

To fall asleep in Christ, then, is to die under His care, with the promise of being raised. Sleep is not an escape from reality but a declaration of confident rest. It is the posture of those who know they will rise.

The nature of the metaphor

Understanding the metaphor of sleep here requires some careful nuance. A metaphor is a comparison that illuminates certain aspects of a reality without equating every single element. When Scripture refers to death as sleep, it is not suggesting that the soul becomes unconscious or inactive. Rather, the metaphor here emphasizes the body's temporary stillness, the peaceful repose of those who have died in Christ, and the certainty of awakening.

One of the most helpful distinctions to make here is between the body and the soul in biblical anthropology. The Scriptures consistently present humans as embodied souls or ensouled bodies.

When death occurs, the body *"sleeps"* in the earth while the soul departs to be with the Lord. The metaphor of sleep thus applies primarily to the body, not the soul.

This is why Paul can say, *"To be away from the body is to be at home with the Lord."* (2 Corinthians 5:8). The soul does not slumber in unconsciousness—it enjoys conscious fellowship with Christ. Yet, the body, whether buried or cremated, is described as being *"asleep,"* awaiting resurrection. This image preserves both the seriousness of death and the hope that believers have in Christ.

Some interpreters have misunderstood this metaphor and used it to support a doctrine of "soul sleep"—the idea that the soul, like the body, becomes unconscious at death and remains so until the resurrection. This idea will be examined more directly in the next chapter. For now, it is essential just to recognize that the metaphor of sleep does not imply soul sleep; it is a pastoral and poetic way of describing the condition of the body and the believer's temporary separation from it.

Moreover, sleep carries with it the implicit idea of rest. *"Blessed are the dead who die in the Lord from now on... they will rest from their labour, for their deeds will follow them."* (Revelation 14:13). Death, for the believer, is not only a sleep but a Sabbath rest. It is a cessation from toil and struggle, a pause in the story while the next chapter awaits. The metaphor is tender, intimate, and deeply hopeful.

The timing and certainty of awakening

Perhaps the most powerful aspect of the sleep metaphor is its inherent connection to awakening. No one falls asleep expecting never to rise again. Sleep is, by nature, a temporary state. It is the anticipation of morning that makes sleep restful. In the same way, the biblical use of sleep to describe death assumes the resurrection as its natural sequel.

Paul underscores this in 1 Corinthians 15:20 when he writes, *"Christ has indeed been raised from the dead, the first fruits of those who have fallen asleep."* The term *"first fruits"* implies a harvest yet to come—those who are asleep will surely follow Christ in resurrection. The metaphor is thus not only descriptive; it is prophetic. It points forward to the great waking day when the trumpet will sound and the dead in Christ will rise.

Daniel offers one of the clearest Old Testament anticipations of this: *"Multitudes who sleep in the dust of the earth will awake: some to everlasting life, others to shame and everlasting contempt."* (12:2). Here again, sleep is used to describe death, and the certainty of resurrection is assumed. The metaphor highlights both the temporary nature of death and the stark dual outcomes: eternal life or judgment.

Jesus, too, speaks of a coming awakening. In John 5:28-29, He declares, *"A time is coming when all who are in their graves will hear his voice and come out."* The voice that once summoned Lazarus from his sleep will one day summon all the dead believers to the resurrection of life, unbelievers to the resurrection of judgment. The metaphor of sleep is therefore not merely a comfort; it is a call to readiness. Only those who sleep in Christ will awaken to eternal joy.

Pastoral power in the sleep metaphor

The pastoral implications of this metaphor are profound. When we stand at the graveside of a loved one who died in Christ, we do not say farewell forever. We say good night. The body rests, like a child tucked into bed, awaiting the dawn. This vision transforms the experience of Christian funerals. The finality of the casket is softened by the assurance that it is not the end.

This imagery is deeply comforting to the grieving. Sleep implies peace, security, and expectation. It encourages believers to view death through the lens of trust. We may not understand all the details of what lies between death and resurrection, but we know the One who holds both. As the hymn puts it, *"Safe in the arms of Jesus, safe on His gentle breast."*

This perspective also calls us to live in anticipation. Just as a good night's sleep is preparation for the day ahead, so the death of a believer is preparation for the glory that awaits. The body rests while the soul enjoys the very presence of Christ, but the full redemption of body and soul is yet to come. In this way, the sleep metaphor sustains hope and reminds us that the story is not finished.

For the early Christians, this metaphor shaped their liturgy and their outlook. Inscriptions on tombs from the catacombs often refer to believers as having *"fallen asleep in the Lord."* This was no sentimental euphemism—it was a bold declaration of faith. Death had been transformed by Christ. What once was terrifying had become peaceful. What once was the end had become a beginning.

Sleep as a reversal of Eden's curse

To appreciate the beauty and depth of the sleep metaphor, we must understand how it operates within the grand arc of redemptive history. Death, introduced in Eden as the result of sin, was the most jarring intrusion into God's good creation. It represented separation, corruption, and judgment. But in Christ, even this most fearsome enemy has been totally defanged. The metaphor of sleep reflects this transformation—not by denying death's reality, but by redefining its meaning for the believer.

In the Garden, God warned Adam that disobedience would lead to death (Genesis 2:17). That warning was fulfilled, not just in physical terms, but spiritually and relationally. Yet the New Testament declares that Christ has reversed this curse through His resurrection. Paul writes in 1 Corinthians 15:26, *"The last enemy to be destroyed is death."* But before its final destruction, death has already been conquered in part—transformed from a tomb to a temporary rest.

When Paul describes believers as those who *"have fallen asleep,"* he is clearly proclaiming that Eden's curse has been decisively challenged. No longer is death the dreaded final word. It has become, in Christ, something far gentler and less permanent. The metaphor of sleep speaks of redemption reaching into the grave itself. It is not just sin and guilt that are dealt with at the cross, but also death's sting. As Paul triumphantly declares, *"Where, O death, is your victory? Where, O death, is your sting?"* (1 Cor. 15:55). This transformation also signals a new creation. Just as sleep precedes waking, so the *"sleep"* of death anticipates resurrection into the new heavens and new earth.

The metaphor is thus not just about rest, but renewal. It hints at the deep rest of Sabbath that will find its ultimate fulfilment in the eternal joy of God's presence. Death is no longer exile — it is homecoming.

Implications for Christian theology and witness

This rich metaphor has implications not only for personal faith but also for Christian theology and our public witness. First, it guards us against two common errors. On one hand, it keeps us from despairing in the face of death. On the other, it prevents us from trivializing death or pretending that it does not matter. To describe death as sleep is to say both that it is real and that it is not final. It affirms the seriousness of mortality while anchoring our hope in resurrection.

Second, the metaphor provides a framework for understanding the intermediate state. As discussed in the previous chapter, believers who die are with Christ, conscious and at peace, but awaiting the resurrection of the body. The metaphor of sleep complements this truth beautifully. The body sleeps while the soul rejoices. This dual reality helps avoid confusion and holds together the biblical tension between "already" and "not yet."

Third, sleep as a metaphor for death challenges the secular narratives of death as being extinction or meaninglessness. The Christian vision of death as sleep is a protest against nihilism. It declares that the dead are not lost in the void, but kept by God, resting until the dawn. This is a powerful testimony in a world increasingly uncertain about what lies beyond. The church, by holding to this metaphor, bears witness to the gospel's victory over death.

Fourth, this metaphor fuels gospel urgency. If death is only a temporary sleep for those in Christ, then the contrast with those outside of Christ becomes even more stark. Jesus said: *"I am the resurrection and the life. The one who believes in me will live, even though they die; and whoever lives by believing in me will never die."* (John 11:25–26).

These are not abstract truths—they are lifelines for a dying world. The metaphor of sleep reveals both the comfort of the gospel and the urgency of our mission.

Comfort in the face of death

Perhaps most importantly, the metaphor of sleep offers deep comfort for the believer and their family. Grief remains, as even Jesus wept at Lazarus' tomb, but it is not grief without hope (1 Thessalonians 4:13). When a loved one in Christ dies, we are not saying goodbye forever—we are whispering, *"Good night."* Their rest is temporary. Morning is coming.

This image has been preserved in countless Christian hymns, poems, and liturgies. Phrases like *"rest in peace"* originate from this biblical metaphor. The earliest Christians carved sleeping metaphors into tombstones, not to romanticize death, but to declare their faith in the One who would awaken them.

Moreover, the metaphor reframes how we approach our own death. Instead of terror, we can face it with peace. To fall asleep in Jesus is to fall into His arms. The One who kept watch over us in life will guard our rest in death. As Psalm says, *"I lie down and sleep; I wake again, because the Lord sustains me."* This psalm speaks of nightly sleep, but it echoes the confidence we carry into the sleep of death.

Even the finality of the grave is softened. Cemeteries become places of waiting. Tombstones and that brass plaque where ashes were scattered, become clear signposts of hope. The church's teaching on sleep as a metaphor for death transforms burial and the scattering of ashes into planting—seeds sown in weakness, raised in glory. As Paul says, *"The body that is sown is perishable, it is raised imperishable."* (1 Corinthians 15:42).

Living in the light of awakening

Finally, the sleep metaphor shapes how we live. If we are destined to awaken, we must live with readiness. Jesus' parables often tie sleep and waking to spiritual watchfulness (e.g., the parable of the ten virgins in Matthew 25).

Believers are not supposed to live in spiritual slumber but in eager anticipation of the Bridegroom's return. The metaphor of death as sleep implicitly calls us to live awake, alert, and devoted to Christ.

It also calls us to comfort one another. The Apostle Paul exhorts the Thessalonian believers, after describing the resurrection of the dead in Christ, to *"encourage one another with these words."* (1 Thessalonians 4:18). That encouragement is grounded in the metaphor of sleep and the promise of waking. The doctrine is not a cold fact — it is warm consolation. To those grieving, it says: *"This is not the end."* And to those facing death, it says: *"Rest is coming. You will not be forgotten. Christ will wake you with a word."*

This metaphor offers not just theological clarity, but spiritual intimacy. It speaks to the childlike trust we are called to embody — a trust that lies down in the grave knowing that our Shepherd will call us by name.

7. THE QUESTION OF 'SOUL SLEEP'

Among the doctrines surrounding Christian death and the afterlife, few have stirred as much confusion and debate as the concept commonly known as *"soul sleep."* This term refers to the belief that when a person dies, their soul becomes unconscious or dormant—entering a state of non-awareness—until the final resurrection. While the body clearly *"sleeps"* in the grave, the question is whether the soul does the same.

Advocates of soul sleep suggest that between death and the resurrection, the dead are not conscious of time, activity, or presence, but instead exist in a suspended, unconscious state. This view is often presented as the straightforward reading of Scriptures that speak of death as *"sleep."* It is also sometimes advanced to resolve the tension between the present experience of death and the finality of resurrection, aiming to preserve the unity of body and soul in the eschatological future.

However, this teaching—although embraced by some Christian groups historically, such as the Seventh-day Adventists and some Anabaptist streams—stands at odds with the mainstream, historical Christian understanding. Throughout Church history, the majority view has been that the soul remains conscious after death, especially for believers, and enters into a provisional state of communion with Christ, awaiting bodily resurrection.

In this chapter we will review all various key biblical passages, theological concerns, and pastoral implications of the soul sleep debate. Our aim is not merely to win an argument, but to better understand the hope Scripture offers to those who die in Christ.

Why the metaphor of sleep is not literal

As discussed in the previous chapter, Scripture often refers to death as *"sleep."* Jesus said of Jairus' daughter, *"She is not dead but asleep."* (Luke 8:52). Concerning Lazarus, Jesus declared, *"Our friend Lazarus has fallen asleep; but I am going there to wake him up."* (John 11:11).

Paul frequently described deceased believers this way: *"Brothers and sisters, we do not want you to be uninformed about those who sleep in death."* (1 Thessalonians 4:13). However, as comforting and poetic as this metaphor may be, it is just that—a metaphor. The metaphor of sleep is employed to convey the temporary nature of death for believers, not to imply unconsciousness of the soul. In everyday speech, we also use euphemisms to soften the impact of death—*"passed away," "at rest,"* or *"gone to sleep"* — not because we are making technical statements about the person's awareness, but because we wish to speak gently about a very painful reality.

As we have already discussed, Jesus Himself used the term *"sleep"* metaphorically. When He said Lazarus was sleeping, the disciples misunderstood Him and thought He meant literal rest. Jesus clarified: *"Lazarus is dead"* (John 11:14). The metaphor of sleep, then, is not a biological or metaphysical statement about consciousness; it is a pastoral expression of hope. It declares that death is not final. But it does not mean that the soul is unaware or inactive.

To base a doctrine of unconsciousness on a metaphor is a poor hermeneutical move. Instead, doctrine must arise from didactic and narrative texts that speak plainly about the soul's condition after death.

Biblical witness to consciousness after death

The overwhelming testimony of the Scriptures is that the soul remains conscious and active after death — particularly for believers. Let us review this again and consider a few key texts.

Jesus and the thief on the cross

Perhaps the most direct refutation of soul sleep comes from Jesus' words to the penitent thief on the cross: *"Truly I tell you, today you will be with me in paradise."* (Luke 23:43). This is not a vague promise of future resurrection. It is an immediate assurance of presence with Christ upon death. The use of the word *"today"* reinforces the immediacy of the experience.

Jesus is not suggesting that the thief will sleep until some distant resurrection morning. He will be with Christ that very day, in a conscious state. Some defenders of soul sleep argue that the punctuation of the verse is mistaken, and that Jesus meant to say, *"Truly I tell you today, you will be with me in paradise [someday]."* But this reading does not fit the natural Greek syntax, nor does it match the urgency and comfort of Jesus' reply to the dying thief. The traditional reading—immediate presence—makes best contextual and grammatical sense.

The rich man and Lazarus (Luke 16:19–31)

In Jesus' parable, both the rich man and the beggar Lazarus die, and both experience conscious realities in the afterlife. Lazarus is comforted *"at Abraham's side,"* while the rich man is in torment. They speak, feel and remember, and they are aware of their surroundings. While some argue this is just a parable and not meant to convey literal details, it still reflects Jesus' assumptions about the afterlife, which would therefore shape His audience's expectations.

Parables often employ real-world settings and truths to make their point. The parable does not depend on an unconscious soul. Quite the contrary, in fact, it presumes full awareness and personal identity after death.

Paul's desire to depart and be with Christ

In Philippians 1:23, Paul writes, *"I desire to depart and be with Christ, which is better by far."* Similarly, in 2 Corinthians 5:8, he says, *"We are confident... and would prefer to be away from the body and at home with the Lord."* In both instances, Paul anticipates an immediate, conscious experience of being with Christ upon death. There is no suggestion that he will fall into unconscious sleep. If death meant unawareness, why would he speak of it as *"better by far"*?

For Paul, to die is gain precisely because it ushers the soul into direct fellowship with Christ. The language is personal and relational, not metaphorical or dormant.

Revelation and the souls under the altar

In Revelation 6:9-10, John sees *"the souls of those who had been slain because of the word of God."* These souls are crying out for justice and vengeance. They are aware of what happened to them, and they engage in speech, emotion, and appeal to God. Though the book of Revelation is largely symbolic, it still reflects a conscious existence between death and resurrection.

The imagery is not of sleeping souls but of waiting, worshiping, and interceding saints. They have memory, voice, and purpose — hardly compatible with the idea of soul sleep.

Doctrinal implications and pastoral concerns

The debate over *"soul sleep"* is not just an academic or theological exercise — it carries profound implications for how we then understand death, hope, comfort, and all Christian doctrine. If believers lapse into unconsciousness until the resurrection, then the emphasis on conscious union with Christ at death is lost. The pastoral promises offered by Jesus and the apostles — of being with the Lord immediately upon death — would need to be reinterpreted or reimagined.

One of the central pastoral concerns is how we comfort those who grieve. Paul's words in 1 Thessalonians 4:13-18 are not just theoretical. They are pastoral balm for aching hearts. *"We do not want you to be uninformed about those who sleep in death,"* he writes, *"so that you do not grieve like the rest of mankind, who have no hope."* He assures them that the dead in Christ will rise, and *"we will be with the Lord forever."*

But that hope begins even before the resurrection. If believers at death immediately enter the conscious presence of Christ — as Jesus said to the thief on the cross — then death becomes not merely the end of earthly life, but the beginning of a deeper communion with Christ. This aligns perfectly with Paul's strong desire to *"depart and be with Christ"* (Philippians 1:23) and the assurance that *"to be away from the body is to be at home with the Lord."* (2 Corinthians 5:8).

The soul sleep view, in contrast, requires either a reinterpretation of these texts or an appeal to anthropological monism (the idea that humans are not made of separable body and soul). Yet this view creates challenges. It diminishes the believer's immediate hope at the point of death and removes the rich theology of the intermediate state where the soul enjoys conscious communion with the risen Christ before the final resurrection.

Furthermore, it poses difficulties for our understanding of Jesus' own experience between death and resurrection. If His human soul was unconscious between Good Friday and Easter Sunday, how are we to interpret His words in Luke 23:46: *"Father, into your hands I commit my spirit"*? Or 1 Peter 3:18-19, which speaks of Him *"being made alive in the Spirit, in which also He went and made proclamation to the imprisoned spirits"*? These texts suggest conscious activity in the intermediate state, not unconscious waiting.

Affirming the Biblical hope

The biblical vision strongly affirms a glorious and hope-filled understanding of life after death: believers, upon death, are immediately ushered into the conscious presence of Christ, where they await the resurrection of the body. This is not speculation—it is the consistent testimony of Scripture.

To die is to be *"with Christ,"* Paul declares, and this is *"better by far."* (Philippians 1:23). The martyr Stephen, as he was being stoned, looked up and saw Jesus standing at the right hand of God, and cried out, *"Lord Jesus, receive my spirit"* (Acts 7:59). These are not the words of a man expecting unconsciousness. They reflect an imminent transition into the personal presence of the Lord.

Revelation 6:9-11 portrays the souls of the martyrs under the altar, crying out to God and receiving comfort and white robes. Again, this imagery assumes conscious awareness, longing, and communion—even before resurrection. If the intermediate state were one of soul sleep, such vivid portrayals of spiritual life would be misleading or inaccurate.

This does not mean we deny the reality of sleep as a metaphor. It remains a beautiful biblical picture for the bodily rest of the believer in the grave, anticipating the resurrection. But it must not be taken as a literal description of the soul's condition. The metaphor comforts the grieving and underscores the certainty of the resurrection—but it never negates the reality of present fellowship with Christ after death.

Conclusion: Living and dying in the light of truth

The doctrine of soul sleep is ultimately incompatible with the full testimony of Scripture. Though it arises from a desire to honour the finality of bodily resurrection and the holistic unity of the person, it does so at the cost of diminishing key biblical promises.

To hold fast to the biblical vision is to proclaim that the believer, at the moment of death, passes immediately into the presence of Jesus—where joy, rest, and conscious communion begin, even as the body sleeps in hope. This assurance changes everything.

It changes how we live. Knowing that Christ is with us in life and will receive us in death shapes our priorities, our courage, and our mission. It changes how we grieve. We sorrow, yes—but not as those without hope. And it changes how we die. In faith. In peace. In the sure hope of seeing our Savior face to face.

This is the truth that comforts the dying, sustains the grieving, and inspires the church. It is not wishful thinking. It is the promise of God, sealed by the resurrection of Jesus Christ—the first fruits of those who have fallen asleep.

8. THE RESURRECTION OF THE DEAD

The resurrection of the dead stands as one of the great pillars of the Christian faith—an event that is not merely symbolic or spiritual, but deeply physical, cosmic, and transformative. It is not a theological footnote, but the very climax of the believer's hope and the final chapter in the story of redemption. Without resurrection, Paul declares, our preaching is useless, and so is our faith (1 Corinthians 15:14). The resurrection is not simply about life after death—it is about life after life after death. It is the moment when death itself is undone, and creation is finally made whole.

The resurrection as Christian hope

Too often, Christian conversations about the afterlife fixate on the intermediate state—the condition of the soul between death and final resurrection. While the intermediate state is very meaningful and comforting, it is not the Christian's ultimate hope. Paul's longing was not to be unclothed, but to be clothed with immortality (2 Corinthians 5:4). Our deepest yearning is not to escape the body, but to receive it back—renewed, glorified, and incorruptible.

In 1 Corinthians 15, Paul launches into one of the most extensive theological expositions in all of Scripture on this topic. His argument hinges on the historical reality of Christ's own bodily resurrection. If Christ has not been raised, then the entire Christian message collapses (1 Corinthians 15:17). But because Christ has been raised, He becomes *"the first fruits of those who have fallen asleep."* (v. 20), a guarantee that those united to Him by faith will likewise rise.

Christ the first fruits

The Apostle's image of *"first fruits"* is drawn from Old Testament agricultural language. The first sheaf of grain offered to God was a pledge of the full harvest to come. So too, Christ's resurrection is not an isolated miracle—it is the beginning of a resurrection harvest that will sweep across all of God's people.

What happened to Jesus is what will happen to every believer: bodily resurrection into eternal glory. This resurrection is not metaphorical or purely spiritual. It is real, tangible, and bodily. After His resurrection, Jesus ate fish with His disciples, showed them His wounds, and declared that a spirit does not have flesh and bones, as they saw He had (Luke 24:39-43). His glorified body, though different in some ways, was continuous with His earthly body. The tomb was empty. The grave clothes were left behind. His body had not been discarded but transformed.

So too, our future resurrection will not consist of discarding our earthly frame like a shell but having it gloriously remade. Paul compares it to a seed being sown: *"It is sown a natural body; it is raised a spiritual body."* (1 Corinthians 15:44). This does not mean the resurrected body is non-physical; rather, it means it will be fully animated and empowered by the Spirit, no longer subject to weakness, decay, or death.

A mystery revealed

Paul calls this a mystery—something once hidden but now revealed. *"Listen, I tell you a mystery: We will not all sleep, but we will all be changed."* (1 Corinthians 15:51). In a moment, in the twinkling of an eye, the dead will be raised imperishable, and we will be transformed. This resurrection event will be sudden, glorious, and universal for those in Christ.

It is important to note that resurrection is not merely about the survival of the soul. Many religions believe in some kind of afterlife or spiritual continuation. But resurrection is unique to biblical Christianity. It is the total reconstitution of the whole person—body and soul—in a renewed creation. This hope is not based on abstract optimism but on the concrete historical event of Jesus rising from the dead. Because He lives, we too shall live.

The voice of the Archangel

In 1 Thessalonians 4:13-18, Paul provides further pastoral clarity for believers grieving those who have died. He writes not to remove sorrow, but to infuse it with hope.

"We do not want you to be uninformed about those who sleep in death," he says, *"so that you do not grieve like the rest of mankind, who have no hope."* (v. 13).

Paul assures them that those who have died in Christ will not be forgotten or left behind. *"The Lord himself will come down from heaven, with a loud command, with the voice of the archangel and with the trumpet call of God, and the dead in Christ will rise first."* (v. 16).

Resurrection is not a private, silent affair—it is a cosmic event, a royal procession. Christ returns not as a gentle teacher but as the triumphant King, reclaiming His people from the grave.

Following the resurrection of the dead, those who are still alive will be caught up together with them *"in the clouds to meet the Lord in the air."* (v. 17). This passage has sometimes been misunderstood as describing a permanent evacuation from the earth. In context, however, the imagery is drawn from ancient customs where citizens would go out to greet a visiting dignitary and escort him back into the city. Paul's language suggests not a departure from earth, but the return of Christ to reign in fullness—and the resurrection saints rising to welcome Him.

The defeat of death

The resurrection of the dead is the final defeat of death. As Paul triumphantly proclaims, *"Death has been swallowed up in victory."* (1 Corinthians 15:54). The last enemy to be destroyed is death itself. It is not merely reversed or sidestepped—it is vanquished. The resurrection means the curse of Genesis 3 is undone, not in part, but in full. The dust of death is not our final state; glory is. This vision has ethical and spiritual implications.

Paul ends his great resurrection chapter not with speculative theology but with a call to action: *"Therefore, my dear brothers and sisters, stand firm. Let nothing move you. Always give yourselves fully to the work of the Lord."* (v. 58). The resurrection is not only future hope—it is present motivation. Knowing that our labour is not in vain, we press on with perseverance, holiness, and purpose.

Resurrection and the restoration of creation

The resurrection of the dead is not an isolated event pertaining only to human destiny. It is inseparably linked to the renewal of all creation. The apostle Paul teaches that the entire created order is groaning as in the pains of childbirth, awaiting liberation from decay (Romans 8:19-23). The resurrection of believers is the first visible sign that the curse is being reversed, and it signals the arrival of God's new creation.

"For the creation waits in eager expectation for the children of God to be revealed," Paul writes. *"The creation itself will be liberated from its bondage to decay and brought into the freedom and glory of the children of God."* (Romans 8:19,21).

The bodily resurrection of God's people, therefore, is not simply about individual restoration—it is about cosmic restoration. Our resurrection is the prelude to the resurrection of the world. As our bodies are redeemed, so too is the earth made new.

This is the great harmony of Scripture's eschatological vision. In Revelation 21, the holy city—the New Jerusalem comes down from heaven to earth. God makes His dwelling with humanity. Heaven does not remain an abstract spiritual realm; it invades and transforms the physical realm. This is resurrection hope: not escape from the world, but the rebirth of the world.

Misconceptions about resurrection

Despite the clarity of Scripture on this subject, many Christians have inherited a diminished view of the afterlife that neglects or misunderstands the resurrection of the body. For some, the resurrection has been replaced with a vague idea of going to heaven as disembodied spirits. For others, it is conflated with reincarnation or absorbed into a general "spiritual continuity."

But resurrection, as taught in the Bible, is unique. It is neither resuscitation nor reincarnation. Resuscitation is the return to mortal life, subject again to death (as in the case of Lazarus). Resurrection is the transformation into an incorruptible state.

Reincarnation posits the recycling of the soul into new bodies over time, a concept foreign to biblical revelation. The Christian doctrine of resurrection affirms the continuity of the individual person and the body, transformed by God's power.

This body-soul unity is crucial. We are not souls trapped in bodies, as some Greek philosophies would suggest. We are embodied beings—flesh and spirit together, and our ultimate hope lies not in shedding the body but in its redemption. Paul underscores this in Philippians 3:20-21: *"We eagerly await a Savior from there, the Lord Jesus Christ, who, by the power that enables him to bring everything under his control, will transform our lowly bodies so that they will be like his glorious body."*

This transformation will be radical. The new body will be imperishable, glorious, powerful, and spiritual—not in the sense of being intangible, but in the sense of being fully animated by God's Spirit. The mortal will put on immortality. What was sown in dishonour will be raised in glory.

Resurrection and justice

The resurrection of the dead is not just a comforting doctrine—it is a message of divine justice. God will not let death have the final word. The wicked may seem to prosper and the righteous to suffer, but the resurrection levels the playing field. It is God's vindication of those who trusted in Him.

Jesus Himself spoke of a resurrection *"of the righteous and the wicked."* (John 5:29). Daniel 12:2 foreshadows this truth: *"Multitudes who sleep in the dust of the earth will awake: some to everlasting life, others to shame and everlasting contempt."* The final resurrection is not only a restoration—it is a reckoning. It affirms that what we do in the body matters, and that God will bring every act to judgment, whether good or evil.

This eschatological justice comforts the oppressed and humbles the proud. It is not the powerful, the wealthy, or the well-connected who will inherit the kingdom, but the meek, the persecuted, and the faithful.

The resurrection reorders our moral universe. What appears weak and foolish now—faith, humility, sacrifice—will shine with glory in the age to come.

Resurrection and Christian worship

The resurrection is not merely a future event to be studied—it is a present reality to be celebrated. Every Lord's Day, the church gathers not simply out of routine but in recognition of resurrection. Sunday is the first day of the week—the day Jesus rose from the dead—and the Christian calendar is forever oriented around this seismic event.

Baptism itself is a resurrection symbol. As Paul writes in Romans 6:4, *"We were therefore buried with him through baptism into death in order that, just as Christ was raised from the dead through the glory of the Father, we too may live a new life."* The act of immersion and rising is not merely symbolic—it is a participation in the dying and rising of Christ. Resurrection hope is embedded in our most foundational practices.

The Lord's Supper also points forward to the resurrection. As we proclaim the Lord's death, we do so *"until he comes."* Each communion meal is a rehearsal for the marriage supper of the Lamb (Revelation 19:9), when the risen Christ will feast with His resurrected bride.

In song, in sacrament, and in liturgy, the church bears witness to the resurrection not as a myth or a metaphor, but as the heartbeat of our faith. We sing not just of a cross, but of an empty tomb. We follow not a dead teacher, but a living King.

Living as resurrection people

The resurrection of the dead is not only a doctrine to affirm—it is a lifestyle to embody. Paul's great resurrection chapter ends with this exhortation in 1 Corinthians 15:58: *"Therefore, my dear brothers and sisters... Always give yourselves fully to the work of the Lord, because you know that your labour in the Lord is not in vain."*

The resurrection fuels perseverance. If death is not the end, then no effort for Christ is wasted. If glory lies beyond the grave, then suffering now is not in vain. We can risk, serve, and sacrifice with open hands, knowing that the eternal weight of glory will far outweigh our present trials (2 Corinthians 4:17).

This hope also inspires holiness. In 1 John 3:2-3, the apostle writes, *"When Christ appears, we shall be like him… All who have this hope in him purify themselves, just as he is pure."* The resurrection calls us to live now in the light of what we will be then. We are not merely biding our time—we are being conformed to the image of Christ, preparing to reign with Him.

Finally, the resurrection drives mission. We proclaim the gospel not as good advice but as world-altering news: Christ is risen, and He will raise us too. This message carries urgency and power. The world is not circling the drain—it is awaiting transformation. The fields are white for harvest, and the King is coming.

Paul's emphasis on resurrection in 1 Corinthians 15 isn't just theological; it's deeply pastoral. His conclusion in verse 58 is resounding: *"Therefore, my dear brothers and sisters, stand firm. Let nothing move you. Always give yourselves fully to the work of the Lord, because you know that your labour in the Lord is not in vain."*

This resurrection hope is not an abstract doctrine to be admired at a distance—it's the foundation for perseverance, holiness, and mission. It's the knowledge that what we do here and now—though subject to decay, opposition, and even death—will not be wasted. The God who raises the dead will redeem every act of faithful service.

Resurrection shapes Christian mission

This eschatological hope directly shapes our mission in the world. The resurrection of the body is not a peripheral promise; it affirms that matter matters, that bodies matter, that creation matters. Christianity does not teach escape from the world, but the renewal of all things.

And so our work—whether preaching, caregiving, creating art, seeking justice, or loving the least—is not just preparation for heaven but participation in the future kingdom.

Paul's resurrection theology profoundly influences his missional outlook. His unrelenting commitment to gospel proclamation—even in the face of suffering and death—makes sense only in light of resurrection. As he says in 1 Corinthians 15:19, *"If only for this life we have hope in Christ, we are of all people most to be pitied."* But because Christ has been raised, Paul is emboldened to suffer, to risk, to spend himself entirely for the sake of the gospel. The resurrection is his motivation for mission, his courage in suffering, and his confidence in eternal reward.

Similarly, in 2 Corinthians 4-5, Paul says, *"We do not lose heart. Though outwardly we are wasting away, yet inwardly we are being renewed day by day... For we know that the one who raised the Lord Jesus from the dead will also raise us with Jesus."* (4:16,14). Our frailty, aging, and eventual death are not causes for despair, because they are caught up in the grand reversal of resurrection. This is not denial of suffering; it is hope in the midst of it.

The bodily continuity and transformation

A frequent question arises: What kind of body will we have in the resurrection? Paul anticipates this in 1 Corinthians 15:35: *"But someone will ask, 'How are the dead raised? With what kind of body will they come?'"* His response is both metaphorical and majestic. He uses the analogy of a seed: *"What you sow does not come to life unless it dies. When you sow, you do not plant the body that will be, but just a seed..."* (v. 36-37). The seed and the plant are continuous but different—the same organism but in a transformed state.

This analogy is so crucial. The resurrection body is not a replacement body, but a glorified continuation. As Paul says, *"So will it be with the resurrection of the dead. The body that is sown is perishable, it is raised imperishable... it is sown in weakness, it is raised in power..."* (v. 42-43). Our future resurrection body will be physical, tangible, yet no longer subject to decay, pain, or sin.

This affirms the goodness of embodiment without the limitations of fallen nature. Moreover, Paul speaks of this resurrected body as *"spiritual"* (v. 44), but he does not mean *"non-physical."* Rather, the term *pneumatikos* refers to a body animated and empowered by the Holy Spirit, as opposed to a body animated by natural life (*psychikos*). Jesus' own resurrection provides the pattern: he ate with the disciples, bore physical wounds, and yet appeared in locked rooms and ascended into heaven. His body was transformed, but still recognizably him.

This continuity assures us that in the resurrection, we will still be ourselves—renewed, perfected, and finally made whole. Our memories, personalities, even our relationships will carry forward, not in the exact form they had on earth, but in glorified, sanctified continuity. Resurrection is not annihilation and recreation, but restoration and transformation.

Victory over death

At the heart of the resurrection promise is the final defeat of death. Paul crescendos in 1 Corinthians 15:54-55: *"Death has been swallowed up in victory. 'Where, O death, is your victory? Where, O death, is your sting?'"* These words echo Isaiah 25 and Hosea 13, connecting the resurrection of believers to the broader prophetic vision of God's triumph over the grave.

For too long, death has been the tyrant—separating loved ones, cutting short lives, mocking human strength. But in Christ, death is a defeated enemy. Already dethroned by the cross and Christ's resurrection, death will be completely destroyed at the final resurrection. *"The last enemy to be destroyed is death,"* Paul declares (v. 26), and the resurrection of the dead is the moment when that destruction is made manifest.

This victory over death also reframes the Christian attitude toward dying. We do not minimize its pain or deny its grief, but we also do not fear it. Because Christ lives, we shall live. Because he rose bodily, so shall we. Because death is not the end, but a door to resurrection life, we face it not with despair, but with defiant hope.

The cosmic implications

The resurrection of the dead is not just about individual bodies. It is a cosmic declaration. Romans 8 tells us that creation itself is groaning, waiting for the *"revealing of the sons of God,"* and that it too *"will be liberated from its bondage to decay and brought into the freedom and glory of the children of God."* (vv. 19, 21). So, the resurrection of human beings is the beginning of a renewed creation. It signals the reversal of the fall, the undoing of decay, and the beginning of new creation.

This means that resurrection is not merely eschatological, but ecological and cosmic. The same power that raised Christ from the dead will renew the heavens and the earth. Christians are therefore not escapists, but stewards of creation. Resurrection affirms our physicality and the enduring value of creation in God's plan.

Living in the power of the resurrection

If the resurrection is our final hope, it is also our present power. Paul writes in Philippians 3:10-11, *"I want to know Christ – yes, to know the power of his resurrection and participation in his sufferings, becoming like him in his death, and so, somehow, attaining to the resurrection from the dead."* This paradox — suffering and resurrection, death and life — is the very shape of Christian discipleship.

We are called to live as Easter people in a Good Friday world. That means dying to self, walking in holiness, loving sacrificially, and witnessing boldly—because we know how the story ends. The resurrection of the dead is not wishful thinking; it is the unshakable promise of God, grounded in the historical resurrection of Christ and guaranteed by the indwelling Spirit who is the down payment of our inheritance.

Paul ends 1 Corinthians 15 not with abstract theology but with a call to action: *"Therefore... stand firm... always give yourselves fully to the work of the Lord."* (v. 58). The resurrection empowers faithfulness today because it assures us that nothing done for Christ is ever wasted.

9. THE NEW HEAVENS AND NEW EARTH

The longing for home

From the dawn of history, the human heart has yearned for something more—something beyond the pain, decay, and sorrow that define life in this broken world. From the patriarchs of Israel who wandered as strangers in the land of promise, to the early Christians who suffered persecution under the Roman Empire, the people of God have always been forward-looking.

This longing is not merely for escape but for fulfilment—for restoration, for resurrection, for renewal. The promise of the new heavens and the new earth is the ultimate expression of that longing finally satisfied.

The biblical vision of hope is not an ethereal escape to some kind of disembodied heaven, rather it's the glorious arrival of God's kingdom in its fullness: a new creation. The book of Revelation culminates not with souls ascending to a celestial realm, but with heaven descending to earth—God making His dwelling with humanity. This eschatological hope gives shape to Christian endurance, worship, and mission. It reorients our imagination and anchors our suffering in the promise of joy.

A renewed creation, not a replacement

Revelation 21 opens with John's breathtaking vision: *"Then I saw a new heaven and a new earth, for the first heaven and the first earth had passed away..."* This language draws heavily from Isaiah 65:17 and Isaiah 66:22, where the prophet speaks of God's coming redemptive work in cosmic terms. The *"new"* heaven and earth are not otherworldly or alien; they are a renewed reality, where what was old is transformed, healed, and made perfect.

The Greek word for *"new"* here is *kainos*, which means new in quality, not in kind. It's not that God is scrapping the original design and starting over with something else, but that He is restoring creation to its intended glory—free from the curse of sin and death.

Just as our resurrection bodies will be recognizably ours, yet glorified and imperishable, so too the new creation will be both continuous with and gloriously transformed from the current one.

This matters deeply. It affirms that God values His creation and intends to redeem it. The Christian hope is not about abandoning the world, but seeing it healed. Paul writes in Romans 8 that *"the creation itself will be liberated from its bondage to decay and brought into the freedom and glory of the children of God."* Creation groans now — but it groans in anticipation, not despair.

The dwelling place of God is with man – forever

Perhaps the most stunning declaration in Revelation 21:3 is this: *"Look! God's dwelling place is now among the people, and He will dwell with them."* This is not a return to Eden — it is something better. The tabernacle and temple hinted at it. The Incarnation fulfilled it in part. But now, in the new creation, the divine presence is fully, permanently among us. *"They will be his people, and God himself will be with them and be their God."*

In this moment, the covenantal promise echoing from Genesis to Revelation comes to consummation. No longer is God hidden behind a veil, approached through mediators. There is no more temple in this city, for *"the Lord God Almighty and the Lamb are its temple."* (Revelation 21:22). The distinction between sacred and secular space vanishes. All of life is holy. All of creation is God's sanctuary.

The implications are staggering. The presence of God is not just a future reality — it becomes the very atmosphere of our eternal existence. Joy, peace, worship, and communion are no longer moments we glimpse by faith; they become the eternal norm.

At the heart of the biblical vision for the new heavens and new earth is the abiding presence of God with His people. Revelation 21:3 declares with resounding clarity: *"Look! God's dwelling place is now among the people, and he will dwell with them. They will be his people, and God himself will be with them and be their God."*

This verse does not merely describe proximity; it describes deep covenantal intimacy restored to its fullest expression. This is Eden regained and now glorified. The long exile of humanity, estranged from the presence of God due to sin, will come to a permanent end.

This final union with God marks the culmination of the divine promise that has echoed through the pages of Scripture. From the tabernacle in the wilderness to the temple in Jerusalem, from the incarnation of Christ to the indwelling of the Holy Spirit in the church, God has progressively drawn closer to His people. But in the new creation, the limitations of each of these previous expressions are totally swept away. No longer will God dwell in shadows or mediated forms—He will dwell in unveiled glory among His redeemed. As Revelation 22:4 affirms, *"They will see his face."*

In a very real sense, this is what makes the new creation truly heaven. Heaven is not merely a place of beauty, peace, or reunion with loved ones, though it will be all of those. Heaven is where God is. To dwell with Him is the very goal and longing of every regenerated heart. The Christian's hope is not floating in a vague, otherworldly realm, but of seeing God and living in His presence in a renewed, resurrected body, in a real and redeemed world.

No more curse

Revelation 22:3 tells us, *"No longer will there be any curse."* This concise statement signals the complete reversal of Genesis 3. The effects of the Fall—sin, death, decay, disease, relational strife, and separation from God—will be entirely removed. The curse was the great unravelling of creation; its removal is the great healing. This is more than a reset—it is the consummation of redemption. Christ's victory is not just over sin in the heart, but over every consequence of sin in creation.

This is why Paul could write in Romans 8:19 that creation itself waits *"in eager expectation for the children of God to be revealed ..."* because *"creation itself will be liberated from its bondage to decay and brought into the freedom and glory of the children of God."* (v. 21).

The new heavens and new earth will not bear the scars of sin's dominion. Nothing unclean, broken, unjust, or fading will remain. Every tear wiped away, every sorrow undone. This vision confronts our tendency to spiritualize salvation in a disembodied way. The gospel is not merely about inner peace or moral improvement. It is about the total restoration of God's good creation. The physical world matters. Our bodies matter. History matters. Redemption is cosmic in scope, and the new creation is the ultimate evidence of God's refusal to surrender anything He has made to sin and death.

No more death, mourning, crying, or pain

The promise continues: *"He will wipe every tear from their eyes. There will be no more death or mourning or crying or pain..."* (Revelation 21:4). These words are among the most beloved in all of Scripture, and for good reason. Every wound, every heartbreak, every injustice, every form of suffering that has ever haunted human life is decisively ended. The things that marked the old order—sickness, grief, and tragedy—will not pass into eternity. They are left behind with the former things.

Importantly, this hope is not abstract. The wiping of tears is an intimate act, not a mechanical reset. God does not merely erase sorrow; He personally addresses it. The God who counts our tears in this life (Psalm 56:8) is the same God who will wipe them away in the next. His justice is not merely judicial—it is also deeply pastoral.

The hope of the Christian Is not that we forget our pain but that it is redeemed. The scars may remain, but they will no longer ache. The story of our lives, with all its wounds and sorrows, will be woven into the greater story of God's grace. What once seemed meaningless will shine with purpose.

The city of God: beauty, light, and life

John's vision is rich with architectural imagery. He sees the New Jerusalem *"coming down out of heaven from God, prepared as a bride beautifully dressed for her husband."* (Revelation 21:2).

The city is radiant with the glory of God. Its gates are always open. Its streets are gold, its foundations adorned with jewels. These images are symbolic, yes, but they speak of an aesthetic and moral beauty beyond compare.

In the ancient world, cities were symbols of security, belonging, and culture. For the early Christians — many of whom were poor, displaced, or persecuted — the image of a glorious heavenly city represented permanence, dignity, and safety. Hebrews 11 tells us that Abraham was looking forward to *"the city with foundations, whose architect and builder is God."* That city is now revealed.

The river of life flows from the throne of God and of the Lamb (Revelation 22:1), and on either side stands the tree of life, bearing fruit in every season. This is the garden of Eden restored and surpassed. Humanity is no longer barred from the tree of life but invited to partake of it forever. The water of life and the tree of life together symbolize abundance, vitality, and unending communion with God.

Worship, work, and the fulfilment of purpose

Many Christians unconsciously assume that eternity will be a never-ending church service in the sky. But the Bible's vision is far richer and more compelling. The new creation will be a place of worship, yes — but worship in its fullest sense: every moment, every activity, every relationship imbued with the glory of God.

In Revelation 22:3, we are told *"his servants will serve him."* This word — serve — is the same used of priestly service in the temple. It includes both worship and work. Humanity was created to rule and steward creation under God (Genesis 1:28), and this mandate is never rescinded — it is restored and fulfilled in the new creation. We will reign with Christ (Revelation 22:5), not in tyranny, but in perfect harmony with God's will.

What will this look like? Scripture gives glimpses but not exhaustive details. Perhaps we will build, create, explore, plant, compose, and invent — without futility, frustration, or pride.

Perhaps we will learn and grow in our knowledge of God and His universe, forever deepening our wonder and worship. What is clear is that the new creation will not be static or dull. It will be a realm of joy, purpose, and fulfilment. As C.S. Lewis imagined, it will be *"further up and further in"* – a never-ending journey into the life of God.

Reunion and redemption

The new creation also brings the hope of reunion with those who have died in Christ. Paul encourages the Thessalonians (4:17). Not to grieve like those who have no hope, because when Christ returns, *"we who are still alive...will be caught up...to meet the Lord in the air. And so we will be with the Lord forever."* This *"we"* includes the living and the dead in Christ—united in one glorious company, not just as souls, but as resurrected people.

This reunion is not the ultimate hope, but it is a precious one. Those who have wept at gravesides, who have longed for one more conversation, one more embrace, find in the gospel the promise of restoration. But even more than that, they find the promise that their loved one will not merely be remembered or spiritually present, but physically alive and glorified in the new creation. The tears of grief will be turned to tears of joy. The broken circle will be mended.

And not only will relationships be restored, but the story of our lives will be redeemed. Every loss, every sorrow, every injustice will be swallowed up in God's perfect justice and joy. The sufferings of this present time, Paul says in Romans 8:18, are not worth comparing with the glory that will be revealed in us. This is not a denial of pain, but its ultimate healing. In the new heavens and new earth, nothing will be wasted. All things will be made new.

The hope that transforms the present

The vision of the new heavens and new earth is not a theological appendix to the gospel—it is its crescendo. It shapes the entire Christian life.

This hope is not a passive escape from the world's pain but a call to faithful endurance, joyful anticipation, and holy living. As Peter exhorts in 2 Peter 3:13-14, *"In keeping with his promise we are looking forward to a new heaven and a new earth, where righteousness dwells. So then…make every effort to be found spotless, blameless and at peace with him."* The future shapes the present. Because we know where history is headed, we live differently now.

We therefore do not despair, even in the face of death. We do not compromise, even in a decaying world. We do not cling to the passing things of this age. We press forward; eyes fixed on the coming kingdom. As Paul declared in 1 Corinthians 15:58, after his great defence of the resurrection: *"Therefore, my dear brothers and sisters, stand firm. Let nothing move you. Always give yourselves fully to the work of the Lord, because you know that your labour in the Lord is not in vain."*

That promise—*"not in vain"*—only makes sense if there is a future. And there is. The Christian's final hope is not merely to die and go to heaven, but to live and reign in a renewed creation, forever with Christ. This is the promise of the gospel. This is the destiny of the redeemed.

10. JUDGMENT, JUSTICE AND JOY

The certainty of Divine judgment

In every human heart, there resides an innate sense that justice must prevail. We see it in the toddler who cries, *"That's not fair!"* and in the nations that rise in protest against oppression and corruption. This longing for justice echoes something deeper than social norms—it reflects the very character of God, who is perfectly just, righteous, and true. Scripture reveals that history is not cyclical or aimless, but linear, progressing toward a divinely appointed conclusion: the final judgment. This is not merely a theological concept; it is an unavoidable appointment for all humanity.

In Acts 17:31, the apostle Paul declared in Athens, *"For He has set a day when He will judge the world with justice by the man He has appointed. He has given proof of this to everyone by raising him from the dead."* The resurrection of Jesus is not only the foundation of Christian hope; it is also God's assurance to the world that judgment is coming and that the Judge has been appointed. Jesus Christ, crucified and risen, will stand as the arbiter of all history.

Unlike human courts—where evidence may often be hidden, motivations misjudged, and outcomes corrupted by bias—the judgment of God will be entirely just. *"He will bring to light what is hidden in darkness and will expose the motives of the heart."* (1 Corinthians 4:5). The final judgment will not merely assess outward behaviour but will unveil the deepest intentions of every soul. Nothing will be overlooked or misunderstood. This is both a cause for holy fear and deep comfort.

For the righteous, this day is not one of dread, but of vindication. For the wicked, it is not a myth, but a promised reckoning. The certainty of this judgment underscores the urgency of the gospel. The cross stands at the centre of this cosmic courtroom, offering pardon to all who place their faith in Christ. Yet those who reject Him choose instead to bear the full weight of their deeds before the throne of justice.

The nature and scope of the judgment

The final judgment is depicted in Scripture with vivid imagery, particularly in Revelation 20. The apostle John writes: *"Then I saw a great white throne and Him who was seated on it. The earth and the heavens fled from His presence, and there was no place for them. And I saw the dead, great and small, standing before the throne, and books were opened."* (Revelation 20:11-12). This throne scene serves to underscore both the majesty of the Judge and the universal scope of His verdict.

All people—regardless of stature, status, or power—will stand before God. This includes the righteous and the unrighteous, the believer and the unbeliever. The *"books"* signify a record of every life, and the *"book of life"* contains the names of those redeemed by the Lamb.

Judgment is based on both works and grace. *"The dead were judged according to what they had done as recorded in the books."* (v.12). Yet the decisive factor is whether one's name is written in the book of life (v.15).

This dual reality reveals the justice and the mercy of God. No injustice will go unpunished, and yet no sin is beyond God's forgiveness for those who are in Christ. The deeds of our lives matter—not in order to secure salvation, but as evidence of the transformation wrought by grace. Faith alone justifies, but faith never remains alone. It bears fruit, and this fruit will be weighed at the judgment seat of Christ.

For believers, this judgment is not punitive but evaluative. Paul describes it this way: *"For we must all appear before the judgment seat of Christ, so that each of us may receive what is due for the things done while in the body, whether good or bad."* (2 Corinthians 5:10). This is not a judgment unto condemnation—*"There is now no condemnation for those who are in Christ Jesus."* (Romans 8:1)—but a judgment unto reward or loss of reward (1 Cor. 3:12-15). God is not merely interested in saving souls but in crowning faithful servants. Every act of obedience, every sacrifice made for His kingdom, will be remembered and rewarded.

The justice of God vindicated

Throughout history, people have questioned the justice of God. Why do the wicked prosper? Why do the innocent suffer? Why does evil seem to go unchecked? The final judgment is God's definitive answer to these agonizing questions. It is His public declaration that every moral account will be settled. The psalmists often wrestled with this tension. Psalm 73 laments the ease of the wicked until the psalmist enters the sanctuary and perceives their final destiny: *"Surely you place them on slippery ground; you cast them down to ruin."* (Psalm 73:18). The problem of evil is not ignored by Scripture but placed within the broader horizon of God's justice. The final judgment is where the balance is made right.

God's justice is not arbitrary or cold. It flows from His holy character and is always exercised in perfect righteousness. *"He will judge the world in righteousness and the peoples with equity."* (Psalm 98:9). The cross of Christ is the ultimate demonstration of this justice, where mercy and judgment met. God did not overlook sin; He bore it. Christ became the lightning rod of God's wrath so that believers could be clothed in His righteousness.

At the final judgment, this righteousness will be on full display. The redeemed will stand not in their own merit but in the merit of Christ. Their sins, though many, have been nailed to the cross, and their names are recorded in the Lamb's book of life. Their good works will shine like stars—not as grounds for salvation, but as trophies of grace. This judgment also vindicates the suffering of the faithful. Those martyred for their testimony, those maligned for their obedience, those who chose the narrow path—all will hear the words, *"Well done, good and faithful servant."* (Matthew 25:21). The tears of injustice will be wiped away by the hands of justice fulfilled.

Joy in the face of judgment

It may seem paradoxical to speak of joy in the context of judgment, but for the Christian, the final judgment is not merely a day of reckoning—it is a day of rejoicing.

The Psalmist declares, *"Let the heavens rejoice, let the earth be glad… He comes to judge the earth. He will judge the world in righteousness and the peoples in His faithfulness."* (Psalm 96:11,13). Judgment is cause for celebration because it means the end of evil, the triumph of good, and the dawning of unending peace.

In John's revelation, following the judgment, the New Jerusalem descends from heaven. God dwells with His people. There is no more death, mourning, crying, or pain. *"The old order of things has passed away."* (Revelation 21:4). The judgment is the doorway to this renewal. It is the necessary prelude to paradise.

For believers, the judgment seat of Christ is really a place of affirmation. Not because of their flawless record, but because of Christ's perfect righteousness imputed to them. The believer's confidence on that day rests in the promises of God. *"This is how love is made complete among us so that we will have confidence on the day of judgment: In this world we are like Jesus."* (1 John 4:17)

This confidence does not breed arrogance, but humble adoration. The awareness that one's sin deserves wrath but has received mercy fuels worship that is deep, joyful, and eternal. As the apostle Paul exclaims in 2 Corinthians 9:15: *"Thanks be to God for His indescribable gift!"* The final judgment is the exclamation point on the gospel story – where the grace of God and the justice of God converge to the glory of God.

A call to live in light of the coming judgment

Knowing that we will stand before the judgment seat of Christ has profound implications for how we live today. It sobers us, sanctifies us, and sends us. Paul writes, *"So we make it our goal to please Him… since we know what it is to fear the Lord, we try to persuade others."* (2 Corinthians 5:9-11). The coming judgment compels both personal holiness and evangelistic urgency. We are not saved by works, but we are saved for good works. The knowledge that our labour in the Lord is not in vain motivates us to abound in service, sacrifice, and obedience. Each act of kindness, each moment of faithfulness, each word of witness – these are not forgotten. They are eternal investments.

Likewise, the final judgment fuels our mission. People matter. Eternity is real. The gospel is urgent. We do not have forever to decide what we believe about Christ. As Paul told the Athenians, God *"commands all people everywhere to repent."* (Acts 17:30). This command is universal, and the time is now.

The final judgment also calls the church to be a witness to righteousness. In a world where truth is often blurred, justice compromised, and sin celebrated, the Church must stand as a prophetic community—pointing to the coming King and the standard of His holiness. The church is not the judge, but it must bear witness to the One who is.

The standard of judgment and the righteousness of God

If God is the Judge of all the earth, the question naturally arises: by what standard will He judge? Scripture is clear that God's judgment is not arbitrary or unpredictable. Rather, it is rooted in His perfect righteousness, His unchanging character, and His revealed will. The God who is holy, just, and true will judge according to truth. This gives both gravity and hope to the doctrine of judgment.

Romans 2:2 reminds us, *"Now we know that God's judgment against those who do such things is based on truth."* This truth is not subject to human variability. It is the eternal, unwavering standard of God's holiness. He judges each person impartially, taking into account not merely external actions but the intentions of the heart (Romans 2:6-11). God is no respecter of persons; He does not favour the religious over the irreligious, the privileged over the poor, or the powerful over the powerless. His judgment is fair, penetrating, and just.

This challenges a popular misconception that judgment will be based on a sliding scale of human morality — that as long as one is *"better than most,"* they'll fare well. But the biblical standard is not comparative morality, but divine righteousness. As Paul writes, *"There is no one righteous, not even one."* (Romans 3:10). All fall short of God's glory, and thus all are without excuse.

The standard is also not merely the written Law of Moses. Even those who did not receive the law will be judged by the law written on their hearts — their conscience bearing witness (Romans 2:14-16). God's judgment is comprehensive and accounts for both revelation and response, action and attitude, knowledge and obedience. This ensures that no one is unjustly condemned or unfairly exonerated.

Judgment through the risen Christ

Crucially, the final judgment will be rendered through Jesus Christ. Paul declared to the Athenians in Acts 17:31, *"For he has set a day when he will judge the world with justice by the man he has appointed. He has given proof of this to everyone by raising him from the dead."* The resurrection is God's validation of Jesus as both Saviour and Judge. The One who bore the sins of the world will be the One before whom the world must stand.

This means that Christ's judgment is not detached from human experience. He was tempted in every way, just as we are, yet without sin. He knows the weakness of the flesh, the allure of sin, and the agony of suffering. Therefore, His judgment is not only righteous but also compassionate. He is not a distant deity dispensing verdicts without understanding; He is the incarnate God who walked among us, full of grace and truth.

The fact that Jesus will be the Judge also reminds us that the gospel is not merely good news of salvation, but a summons to respond. As Jesus Himself said, *"Whoever rejects me and does not accept my words has a judge; the very words I have spoken will condemn them at the last day."* (John 12:48). Christ's words are not suggestions but declarations of divine authority. To embrace or reject Him is to determine one's eternal standing.

The books will be opened

The book of Revelation presents a vivid portrayal of judgment: *"Then I saw a great white throne and him who was seated on it... And I saw the dead, great and small, standing before the throne, and books were opened."* (Revelation 20:11-12).

These *"books"* symbolise the records of human deeds, thoughts, and intentions. Judgment is not random; it is informed by divine knowledge. Every act of injustice, every word of hatred, every moment of unbelief is recorded.

And yet, there is another book — the book of life. *"Anyone whose name was not found written in the book of life was thrown into the lake of fire."* (Revelation 20:15). This is the book of grace, not works; the register of those who belong to Christ, not those who have earned their place through merit.

The dual imagery of the books emphasises the true weight of judgment and the wonder of grace. While all will be judged according to what they have done, only those in Christ are found righteous.

It is sobering to realise that no hidden sin escapes God's notice. Jesus said, *"There is nothing concealed that will not be disclosed or hidden that will not be made known."* (Luke 12:2). Every motive, every whisper, every secret inclination will be brought to light. This is not to terrorise the faithful but to call all people to live in the light of God's holiness, trusting not in their righteousness but in the finished work of Christ.

The justice we long for

Though the prospect of judgment is sobering, it is also deeply hopeful. In a world which is marred by injustice, corruption, and impunity, the promise of divine judgment assures us that evil will not have the last word. Every injustice that escapes human courts will be addressed. Every cry of the oppressed, every sigh of the afflicted, every injustice buried in silence will be answered by the God who sees and knows.

This is why the psalmist can exclaim, *"He will judge the world in righteousness and the peoples with equity."* (Psalm 98:9). Far from dreading God's judgment, the faithful long for it. Not because they are perfect, but because they know the Judge is good. His justice is not retribution for its own sake but the setting right of a broken world.

In the prophetic vision of Isaiah, the coming King is one *"who will judge the needy with righteousness and with justice give decisions for the poor of the earth."* (Isaiah 11:4). This is not the judgment of a tyrant, but of a Shepherd-King who brings equity, restores peace, and vindicates the righteous. It is this hope that energises the Church's mission and sustains our perseverance.

The joy of the redeemed

For those who are in Christ, the anticipation of God's judgment is not a source of dread but of deep and enduring joy. This may seem paradoxical at first. How can joy be found in the day when every thought, word, and deed is laid bare before the all-seeing eyes of God?

The answer lies in the gospel. Because of the finished work of Christ, believers approach the Day of the Lord not with terror, but with reverence and longing.

As Paul writes in Romans 8:1, *"Therefore, there is now no condemnation for those who are in Christ Jesus."* The judgment that once threatened us with eternal separation has already been borne by Christ on the cross. The wrath we deserved was absorbed by Him, and His righteousness has been credited to our account. At the final judgment, the verdict for every believer is already settled: not guilty.

More than that, it is righteous in Christ. This is why Paul can look forward to *"the crown of righteousness, which the Lord, the righteous Judge, will award to me on that day – and not only to me, but also to all who have longed for his appearing."* (2 Timothy 4:8).

This longing—this eager anticipation—is the hallmark of Christian hope. The final judgment is not merely an event of cosmic reckoning; it is the day when justice is fully established, when evil is forever vanquished, and when the faithful are vindicated. It is the day when Christ is revealed in glory and when we, His redeemed people, are revealed with Him (Colossians 3:4). The Judge is also our Savior, and the courtroom is the setting of our public adoption.

Worship in the light of judgment

When we finally grasp the reality of God's coming judgment, it transforms our worship. Throughout Scripture, the judgment of God is a cause for praise. The psalmist calls on creation to rejoice because *"the Lord comes to judge the earth. He will judge the world in righteousness and the peoples in his truth."* (Psalm 96:13).

Judgment is not arbitrary, nor is it capricious — it is the righteous response of a holy God to the brokenness of the world. And because this Judge is also the Redeemer, His justice is inseparable from His mercy.

In Revelation 15, John sees those who have been victorious singing *"the song of God's servant Moses and of the Lamb."* They declare, *"Great and marvellous are your deeds, Lord God Almighty. Just and true are your ways, King of the nations."* (Revelation 15:3). This song is sung in the context of judgment, and it is filled with joy and reverence. The saints praise God not just for His love, but for His justice.

For the Christian, worship is shaped by awe and assurance — by the weight of God's holiness and the wonder of His grace. We worship a God who does not overlook evil, who will right every wrong, and who has made a way for sinners to be justified through faith in Jesus Christ. Our songs, our prayers, our lives — everything we offer in worship — are shaped by the certainty that the world is not spinning aimlessly but moving toward a day of perfect justice and eternal joy.

Living in light of the final judgment

The doctrine of final judgment is not meant to be a theological curiosity or a tool for fear-based motivation. It is a truth that anchors our ethics, our perseverance, and our mission. Knowing that we will give an account spurs us to live with purpose. Paul writes, *"So we make it our goal to please him... For we must all appear before the judgment seat of Christ."* (2 Corinthians 5:9–10). This does not imply a salvation earned by works but a life lived in gratitude for grace.

It also fuels our commitment to justice in this world. If God cares deeply about justice—and if He will bring every injustice to light—then we, too, must reflect that passion in how we treat others. We pursue righteousness not to earn His favour, but because we have received it. Our choices, relationships, and priorities are all reoriented by the reality of the coming Day.

Moreover, the certainty of judgment motivates evangelism. As Paul declares in Acts 17:31, God *"has set a day when he will judge the world with justice by the man he has appointed."*

This knowledge compelled Paul to reason with unbelievers, to plead with them to turn to the risen Christ. So too, it compels us to proclaim the gospel—to invite others into the joy and security of knowing the Judge as Saviour.

Justice and joy embraced together

The Christian faith holds justice and joy together in a way no other worldview can. On one hand, we take evil seriously. We believe in a real judgment, a final reckoning, and a God who will not be mocked. On the other hand, we rejoice, because this God of justice has made a way for mercy to triumph. The cross stands at the intersection of these two realities. There, justice was upheld and love was poured out. There, judgment fell—and joy was made possible.

As we await the final day, we do so not with trembling, but with trust. Not with fear, but with faith. The Judge is also the Lamb. The verdict is secure. The joy is everlasting.

11. SPIRITUAL DEATH AND NEW BIRTH

The biblical story of death is not limited to the grave or the future judgment. At its core, it includes a deeper, and more pervasive reality: spiritual death. This condition, which separates mankind from the life of God, is not a peripheral theological concept but the heart of the human predicament. It is the invisible but devastating result of sin, manifest in alienation, hardness of heart, and rebellion against God. Yet, the gospel proclaims a glorious answer: new birth. To understand the full significance of death in God's kingdom economy and the power of Christ's redemption, we must grasp the meaning and consequence of spiritual death — and the miracle of being made alive in Christ.

Dead in transgressions and sins

Paul's words to the Ephesians are sobering and direct: *"As for you, you were dead in your transgressions and sins."* (Ephesians 2:1). This death is not metaphorical in the sense of being merely symbolic or poetic. It is spiritual death — a real and present separation from the life of God. He goes on to say that this was the state of all humanity, not just a particular group: *"All of us also lived among them at one time, gratifying the cravings of our flesh and following its desires and thoughts."* (Ephesians 2:3).

This is not physical death. The people Paul describes are living, breathing, acting — but spiritually dead. This death does not mean inactivity but separation. Just as physical death is the separation of the soul from the body, so spiritual death is the separation of the soul from God. It is marked by disobedience, bondage to sin, and a life shaped by the world, the flesh, and the devil.

Jesus echoes this condition in John 5:24 when He speaks of passing from death to life: *"Whoever hears my word and believes him who sent me has eternal life and will not be judged but has crossed over from death to life."* Here, "death" is not the end of physical existence but the state of separation from God, and "life" is the restoration of communion with God.

In John 3, Jesus tells Nicodemus that without being born again, no one can even see the kingdom of God. This is not just about entering heaven after death; it's about experiencing a spiritual resurrection now — moving from death to life through the new birth.

The nature of spiritual death

Spiritual death is not merely a passive condition; it is active in its effects. It manifests in rebellion against God, suppression of truth, and a refusal to acknowledge or glorify Him. Paul describes the spiritually dead in Romans 1 as those who *"suppress the truth by their wickedness"* (v.18) and who *"neither glorified him as God nor gave thanks to him."* (v.21). This death is a spiritual inertia — not of inactivity, but of movement in the wrong direction, away from the light of God into deeper darkness.

The spiritually dead are not neutral. They are *"by nature deserving of wrath."* (Ephesians 2:3), enslaved to sin, and under the dominion of the evil one. This is not just about moral weakness but total inability to respond to God without divine intervention. Jesus said in John 6:44, *"No one can come to me unless the Father who sent me draws them."* The spiritually dead need resurrection, not renovation.

This perspective is essential to a biblical anthropology. Mankind is not essentially good but hindered by ignorance or bad habits; we are spiritually dead and in desperate need of life. The gospel is not self-improvement but resurrection. It is not advice, but news — the announcement that in Christ, God has made a way for the dead to live.

The miracle of new birth

Against this dark backdrop, the light of the gospel shines all the more brilliantly. Paul continues in Ephesians 2: *"But because of his great love for us, God, who is rich in mercy, made us alive with Christ even when we were dead in transgressions"* (vv. 4–5). This is the language of spiritual resurrection.

Just as Jesus was raised from the dead physically, so believers are raised spiritually — made alive in union with Him. This new birth is not a human achievement. It is entirely a work of God's mercy and grace. *"It is by grace you have been saved."* (v.5). John declares that those who receive Christ and are born of God are not born *"of natural descent, nor of human decision or a husband's will, but born of God."* (1:13) Jesus told Nicodemus, *"The wind blows wherever it pleases... so it is with everyone born of the Spirit."* (John 3:8). The new birth is a sovereign, Spirit-wrought act of God that brings the dead to life.

This miraculous rebirth is not merely a theological concept; it is a transformation that changes the trajectory of a person's life. Those who were once alienated are reconciled. Those who once walked in darkness now walk in the light. The old has gone; the new has come. As Paul puts it in 2 Corinthians 5:17, *"If anyone is in Christ, the new creation has come: The old has gone, the new is here!"*

If spiritual death is our natural state apart from Christ, then the doctrine of regeneration—what Jesus refers to as being *"born again"* (John 3:3) — is not optional. It is the essential miracle at the heart of salvation. No one enters the kingdom of God without it. Just as our first birth brought us into physical life, so our second birth ushers us into spiritual life. Without this rebirth, we remain spiritually dead—unresponsive, alienated, and incapable of living the life God intends for us.

"You must be born again"

When Jesus spoke to Nicodemus, a learned Pharisee and teacher of Israel, He confronted not ignorance, but blindness. Of course Nicodemus had knowledge of the Scriptures, but not the life they offered. Jesus said plainly: *"Very truly I tell you, no one can see the kingdom of God unless they are born again."* (John 3:3). This phrase *"born again"* could also be translated *"born from above,"* indicating the divine origin of this new birth. Nicodemus was confused. He took Jesus' words literally and asked how a grown man could re-enter his mother's womb. Jesus responded: *"Flesh gives birth to flesh, but the Spirit gives birth to spirit."* (John 3:6).

This rebirth is not physical but spiritual. It is the sovereign work of the Holy Spirit, breathing new life into a soul dead in sin. Just as we played no active role in our physical birth, so our spiritual birth is a gift of grace, not a human accomplishment.

Made alive with Christ

Paul echoes this theme in Ephesians 2, where he describes the movement from death to life. After declaring that we were *"dead in your transgressions and sins,"* he continues: *"But because of his great love for us, God, who is rich in mercy, made us alive with Christ."* (Ephesians 2:4-5). The language is powerful—made alive. We were not merely weak or sickly, but utterly lifeless.

Regeneration is not a spiritual improvement; it is a resurrection. This is why the new birth is more than a metaphor—it is a miracle. In Colossians 2:13, Paul again says, *"When you were dead in your sins... God made you alive with Christ."* This divine intervention restores what was lost in Eden: fellowship with God, spiritual sensitivity, and the ability to truly live. It is the reversal of spiritual death, a foretaste of the resurrection to come.

The role of the Word and Spirit

While regeneration is a work of the Holy Spirit, it is often effected through the Word of God. James writes, *"He chose to give us birth through the word of truth."* (James 1:18), and Peter says, *"You have been born again... through the living and enduring word of God."* (1 Peter 1:23). The Spirit works in concert with the Word, bringing conviction, revelation, and transformation.

This new birth is not the result of moral effort, religious heritage, or personal sincerity. It is the supernatural work of God, awakening a heart that was once stone and making it flesh (Ezekiel 36:26). It creates new desires, new affections, and a new orientation toward God.

As Paul puts it, *"if anyone is in Christ, the new creation has come: The old has gone, the new is here!"* (2 Corinthians 5:17).

Assurance of new life

The evidence of this rebirth is not simply a moment of decision or an emotional experience, but a transformed life. John, in his first epistle, outlines several marks of the new birth: belief in Jesus as the Christ (1 John 5:1), love for God's people (1 John 3:14), victory over sin (1 John 3:9), and obedience to God's commands (1 John 2:29).

Yet this transformation is not instantaneous perfection. It is a process, a journey of sanctification that begins with regeneration. The new life grows, like a seed planted in good soil. It produces fruit over time, cultivated by the Spirit and nourished by the Word. But it is real life, divine life, and its presence assures us that we truly belong to Christ.

While physical death marks the end of earthly life, and eternal death signals final separation from God, the greatest tragedy for humanity may well be spiritual death — a present condition that renders the soul blind, deaf, and unresponsive to the things of God. This reality makes the doctrine of new birth not only important but utterly essential. It is not one spiritual option among many; it is the divine intervention by which the spiritually dead are brought to life in Christ.

Paul describes this supernatural rebirth with breathtaking clarity in Titus 3:5: *"He saved us, not because of righteous things we had done, but because of his mercy. He saved us through the washing of rebirth and renewal by the Holy Spirit."* The imagery here is profound. Rebirth is not some kind of a metaphorical nod to improvement or rehabilitation — it is a creative act of God, parallel to the original creation, in which dead souls are resurrected spiritually and made alive to the reality of God's presence, will, and love.

This spiritual awakening is accompanied by a truly radical reorientation of the heart. Prior to the new birth, the heart is described in Jeremiah 17:9 as, *"deceitful above all things and beyond cure."* In regeneration, that stony heart is replaced with a heart of flesh (Ezekiel 36:26), sensitive and responsive to the Spirit.

This transformation is the fulfilment of the promises God made to His people throughout redemptive history — not merely that they would be forgiven, but that they would be changed.

Jesus made it unmistakably clear: *"No one can see the kingdom of God unless they are born again."* (John 3:3). The kingdom is not merely a place to which people go, but a reality they must enter — and entry requires spiritual rebirth. Without it, we remain outside, no matter how religious or morally upright we appear. The Pharisee Nicodemus was a religious man by every external measure, yet Jesus told him plainly that he needed to be born again. His credentials did not grant him access to the kingdom — only a divine work of renewal could.

This new birth is the work of the Holy Spirit. As Jesus explained to Nicodemus, *"The wind blows wherever it pleases. You hear its sound, but you cannot tell where it comes from or where it is going. So, it is with everyone born of the Spirit."* (John 3:8). There is mystery in the Spirit's movement, but also assurance. Where He works, life follows. Those once dead in sin are awakened to faith, to repentance, and to love for God and neighbour.

The evidence of spiritual rebirth "s no' just doctrinal assent or emotional zeal but a transformed life. John writes, *"No one who is born of God will continue to sin, because God's seed remains in them; they cannot go on sinning, because they have been born of God."* (1 John 3:9). This does not mean that believers attain sinless perfection, but rather that their relationship to sin has changed. They are grieved by it, they resist it, and they are empowered to overcome it through the Spirit.

Moreover, those who are born again demonstrate the fruit of the Holy Spirit: love, joy, peace, forbearance, kindness, goodness, faithfulness, gentleness, and self-control (Galatians 5:22-23). These are not manufactured virtues but the natural outworking of a new nature, cultivated by the Spirit within. They do not appear all at once or in full maturity, but their presence — however small at first — marks the beginning of a sanctifying journey toward Christlikeness.

The implications of spiritual rebirth reach beyond the individual. The Church is composed not of people who merely attend a service or adhere to a set of teachings, but of those who have been born of the Spirit and united to Christ. The Church, then, is the community of the spiritually alive, a fellowship of new creations who bear witness to the power of the gospel.

In this way, spiritual rebirth restores what was lost in Eden — not in full, but as a foretaste of what is to come. Just as Adam and Eve once walked with God in the cool of the day, so now, through new birth, believers walk with God in the Spirit. They hear His voice in His Word, commune with Him in prayer, and grow in likeness to His Son. Though the body remains subject to decay and death, the inner person is being renewed day by day (2 Corinthians 4:16), awaiting the full redemption of both body and soul.

The contrast between spiritual death and new birth could not be starker. One is marked by alienation, darkness, and futility; the other by reconciliation, light, and purpose. One ends in judgment; the other begins in grace and leads to glory. The path from death to life is not one we discover through effort or intellect. It is one we receive as a gift — a gift secured by the death and resurrection of Jesus and applied to us by the Spirit who gives life.

This transformation shapes everything: our identity, our desires, our destiny. We no longer live for ourselves but for Him who died and was raised again. We do not fear death as the end, for we have already passed from death to life. And we face the future not with dread but with hope, knowing that the God who began this work in us will carry it on to completion until the day of Christ Jesus.

12. THE SECOND DEATH AND THE LAKE OF FIRE

The book of Revelation offers some of the most dramatic and sobering depictions of divine judgment in all of Scripture. Among its climactic visions is the harrowing image of the *"second death,"* described in Revelation 20 as the final destination of the devil, his followers, and all whose names are not found in the book of life. This chapter explores the meaning, purpose, and theological implications of the second death, examining how it fits within the broader biblical narrative of justice, mercy, and eschatological hope.

The final judgment and the lake of fire

Revelation 20 presents a vivid scene often referred to as the Great White Throne Judgment. In verses 11–15, the Apostle John describes a moment in which the dead, great and small, stand before the throne of God. *"The dead were judged according to what they had done as recorded in the books."* Then John writes: *"Death and Hades were thrown into the lake of fire. The lake of fire is the second death."* This statement is repeated again in Revelation 21:8 with a list of those who experience this final fate — the cowardly, unbelieving, vile, murderers, sexually immoral, those who practice magic arts, idolaters, and all liars.

The term *"second death"* is unique to Revelation. While physical death is the first death — the common human experience since the fall — the second death represents an ultimate and eternal separation from the presence and blessing of God. It is not merely an extension of physical death, nor is it annihilation in the sense of ceasing to exist. Rather, it is a conscious and irreversible state of judgment.

Theological significance of the second death

The second death signifies the culmination of divine justice. It is the final act in God's judgment against sin and rebellion. While the first death came into the world through Adam's sin, the second death is reserved for those who reject the life offered in Christ.

This is not a random or arbitrary punishment; it is the full and fair outworking of human responsibility in light of the divine revelation and grace. From the outset of Scripture, God reveals Himself as just and holy. The penalty for sin is death (Genesis 2:17; Romans 6:23), and apart from the saving work of Christ, all humanity stands under condemnation.

The lake of fire, therefore, is not merely a punishment but a vindication of God's righteousness and a declaration of His moral order. In a world plagued by evil, injustice, and rebellion, the second death assures us that these things will not go unanswered. Every wrong will be righted, and every injustice addressed.

The destiny of Satan and his followers

Significantly, the first to be consigned to the lake of fire are the devil, the beast, and the false prophet (Revelation 20:10). This triad represents the concentrated forces of deception, rebellion, and evil. Their fate is sealed before the final judgment of humanity. Their punishment is described as torment *"day and night for ever and ever,"* a phrase that underscores the eternal nature of their condemnation.

In Revelation 20:14-15, the focus expands to all the dead who are not found in the book of life. This book, referred to earlier in Revelation (3:5; 13:8; 17:8; 21:27), is symbolic of God's knowledge of those who belong to Him — those redeemed by the blood of the Lamb. The absence of one's name in this book indicates an unredeemed life, unrepentant in sin, and therefore subject to the same judgment as the enemies of God.

The second death and human responsibility

While the imagery of the lake of fire is terrifying, it serves an essential purpose in the biblical narrative: to awaken moral urgency and spiritual seriousness. This doctrine of final judgment, and of the second death in particular, is not meant to paralyze believers with fear but to anchor them in the gravity of their faith. It confronts the complacency that can so easily settle in when eternal realities are neglected.

Throughout the New Testament, the call to repentance is predicated on the reality of the coming judgment. Paul, in addressing the Athenians (Acts 17:31), declares that God *"has set a day when he will judge the world with justice by the man he has appointed."* This future judgment invites a present response. The doctrine of the second death does not simply predict doom — it invites deliverance. It places before every person the choice between life and death, blessing and curse, as Moses did in Deuteronomy 30:19. The sobering truth is that not all will choose life. The second death is the consequence of persistent rejection of God's grace. It is not the desire of God that anyone should perish (2 Peter 3:9), but He honours the free will of those who, in the face of truth and love, choose darkness over light (John 3:19).

The book of life and eternal security

The contrast between those who face the second death and those written in the book of life reveals the centrality of grace in the Christian faith. No one escapes judgment by merit or moral superiority. It is only by being united to Christ — whose name and righteousness secure our place in the book — that we escape the second death.

This truth offers profound comfort to believers. As Jesus said in John 5:24, *"Whoever hears my word and believes him who sent me has eternal life and will not be judged but has crossed over from death to life."* The believer's security rests not in his ability to avoid sin perfectly, but in the finished work of Christ who bore the judgment in our place. While the imagery of the lake of fire is meant to warn, it also functions to exalt the mercy of God. That there is a second death reminds us of how desperately we need a second birth. And the gospel proclaims that such a rebirth is freely offered in Christ.

The finality of the second death

The language of "second death" in Revelation 20:14–15 is deeply sobering: *"Then death and Hades were thrown into the lake of fire. The lake of fire is the second death. Anyone whose name was not found written in the book of life was thrown into the lake of fire."* Here we find a climactic portrayal of God's judgment.

Death itself — along with the intermediate state (Hades) — is done away with, and a final, irreversible fate is assigned to those outside Christ: the second death.

This *"second death"* is not merely physical, as all people die once physically (Hebrews 9:27). It is instead the ultimate separation from God — a spiritual and eternal death. The first death is a consequence of Adam's sin; the second is the result of personal, unrepentant sin and rebellion against God. It is not remedial or purifying, as some theological traditions suggest. It is terminal, definitive, and final.

This final judgment is presented in stark terms in Revelation 21:8: *"But the cowardly, the unbelieving, the vile, the murderers, the sexually immoral ... their place will be in the fiery lake of burning sulphur. This is the second death."* The judgment here is not arbitrary; it is just. It is the culmination of a life lived in persistent resistance to the grace and truth of God. The second death is not simply the extinguishing of existence — it is the full realization of the wages of sin (Romans 6:23).

It is important to understand this not merely as a theological abstraction, but as a terrifying reality that reflects both God's holiness and His justice. While modern sensibilities may recoil at the notion of hell or eternal punishment, the Bible does not soften its language. The second death is a sobering doctrine, designed not to breed fear for its own sake, but to awaken repentance and deepen our appreciation of the gospel.

The book of life and eternal security

The repeated emphasis in Revelation on *"the book of life"* is significant. Those whose names are found in this book are spared from the second death. Revelation 20:15 says, *"If anyone's name was not found written in the book of life, he was thrown into the lake of fire."* This is not a random ledger but a divine record of those united with Christ by faith — those redeemed and sealed for eternity. This imagery is meant to communicate the security of the believer.

The names written in the book of life are written there not because of moral superiority, but because of the grace of God in Christ. As Paul says in Ephesians 1:4, *"He chose us in him before the creation of the world to be holy and blameless in his sight."* The doctrine of election, far from being cold or deterministic, underscores the utter sufficiency of God's mercy in saving sinners.

The believer need not fear the second death. Revelation 2:11 says, *"He who overcomes will not be hurt at all by the second death."* In Christ, we are counted among the overcomers — those who, by faith, endure to the end and are preserved by the power of God. The second death has no claim over those who are in Christ Jesus, for there is now *"no condemnation"* for them (Romans 8:1). Our names are written in heaven, not by our own effort, but by the blood of the Lamb.

The lake of fire: metaphor or reality?

There has been considerable debate throughout church history about the nature of the lake of fire. Is it literal or symbolic? Eternal conscious torment or metaphorical annihilation? These are not just academic questions — they touch on our view of God's justice, mercy, and the seriousness of sin.

Revelation, as apocalyptic literature, makes heavy use of symbolic language. Fire, sulphur, lakes, and thrones are vivid images designed to communicate spiritual truths through sensory terms. However, even if the language is symbolic, the reality it describes is not any less severe. Symbolism in Scripture is often used to amplify reality, not to diminish it. Jesus' own teachings about hell — where *"the worm does not die, and the fire is not quenched."* (Mark 9:48) — align with this depiction of the second death as a place of irreversible judgment.

For some, this leads to the doctrine of annihilationism — the belief that the wicked will ultimately be destroyed and cease to exist rather than suffer eternal conscious torment. They argue that this view better reflects the justice of God and the meaning of the term *"death."*

Others, however, point to texts like Matthew 25:46 — *"Then they will go away to eternal punishment, but the righteous to eternal life"* — to support the traditional doctrine of eternal conscious punishment.

The key point remains: the second death represents ultimate exclusion from the presence of God. Whether conceived as conscious torment or eternal destruction, it is the final and dreadful end for those who reject the gospel. Scripture is less concerned with resolving all our philosophical tensions and more concerned with urging repentance and trust in Christ.

God's justice and mercy held together

One of the most difficult tensions in Christian theology is holding together the justice of God and His mercy. The second death seems at first glance incompatible with the love of God. Yet it is only in the light of God's holiness that His mercy shines most brightly.

The lake of fire Is not the result of divine cruelty but of divine justice. God is not indifferent to evil. He will not allow sin to go unpunished. Every injustice, every rebellion, every ungodly act will be accounted for — either at the cross, where Christ bore the punishment in our place, or in the final judgment. The second death is not God's failure; it is the full revelation of His justice.

At the same time, the fact that any are saved at all is a testimony to the profound mercy of God. No one deserves to have their name in the book of life. Yet, because of Jesus' death and resurrection, countless names are written there. Mercy triumphs over judgment (James 2:13) — not by erasing judgment but by absorbing it through the atoning sacrifice of Christ.

This dual reality should produce in us deep humility. It should kill all spiritual pride and awaken both urgency and gratitude. We preach Christ not merely to improve lives but to save souls from the second death. The gravity of this truth should inform our evangelism, our theology, and our worship.

The gospel as rescue from the second death

The doctrine of the second death is not intended to be a mere theological curiosity. It is a pastoral truth — a call to flee from wrath and to run to Christ. The gospel is, at its core, good news because there is bad news. The bad news is that sin separates us from God, and apart from Christ, we are destined for the second death. The good news is that Jesus has conquered death — both the first and the second — and offers life eternal to all who believe.

This is why the apostles preached with such urgency. Paul wrote in 2 Corinthians 5:20, *"We implore you on Christ's behalf: Be reconciled to God."* He understood that the stakes were not merely temporal but eternal. Every soul hangs in the balance — destined either for eternal life in the presence of God or for the second death, eternally separated from Him.

The gospel is not simply an offer of a better life now. It is deliverance from the dominion of darkness (Colossians 1:13), from sin's penalty (Romans 6:23), and ultimately from the second death. In Christ, we have passed from death to life (John 5:24). This is not poetic metaphor — it is reality. The believer has been rescued, not just from meaningless existence or moral failure, but from the eternal consequences of rebellion against God.

The assurance of salvation does not rest on subjective feelings but on the objective work of Christ. Because He bore our sin, suffered in our place, and rose again in triumph, we can face the prospect of death — even the second death — without fear. *"Whoever believes in the Son has eternal life,"* Jesus said. *"But whoever rejects the Son will not see life, for God's wrath remains on them."* (John 3:36). These are not abstract theological concepts but eternal realities with personal implications.

Evangelism, missions, and eternal consequences

The reality of the second death gives urgency to evangelism. If eternal separation from God awaits those without Christ, then the church cannot be passive.

The lake of fire is not a metaphor to be debated in seminaries alone — it is a biblical truth that should drive our mission and shape our prayers. We do not share the gospel merely to improve society or enhance morality. We do so because people's eternal destinies are at stake.

Jesus spoke more about hell than almost anyone else in Scripture — not to terrify but to warn. His love did not silence truth. In fact, His love compelled Him to speak of judgment in Mark 8:36, *"What good is it for someone to gain the whole world, yet forfeit their soul?"* The gospel is not optional advice for living — it is the only path to escape the second death and receive the gift of eternal life.

For the early church, the prospect of final judgment was a motivating force in missions. Paul's proclamation that *"we must all appear before the judgment seat of Christ."* (2 Corinthians 5:10) was immediately followed by a missionary appeal: *"Since, then, we know what it is to fear the Lord, we try to persuade others."* (v. 11). Evangelism is not a marketing campaign or religious hobby — it is a' act of eternal consequence. We persuade, plead, and proclaim, knowing that the second death is not a metaphorical danger but a spiritual reality.

Even if the modern church is uncomfortable with this doctrine, Scripture does not allow us to remain silent. We must speak the truth in love (Ephesians 4:15), and the truth includes both the mercy of God and the reality of eternal judgment. The most loving thing we can do is tell the whole truth — that there is a hell to shun and a heaven to gain, and Christ is the only way to escape the former and enter the latter.

Worship in light of judgment

Though the second death is a solemn and weighty doctrine, it ultimately exalts the glory of God. Revelation 19 portrays a scene of worship in heaven where the hosts cry, *"Hallelujah! Salvation and glory and power belong to our God, for true and just are his judgments."* (Revelation 19:1-2).

Even God's judgment — including the judgment of the wicked — is part of His praiseworthy holiness. This does not imply that Christians gloat over the lost. There is no room for triumphalism. But it does mean that God's justice is not something to be embarrassed by. His holiness demands that evil be judged. Were God to simply ignore sin or sweep it under the cosmic rug, He would cease to be just. The cross of Christ demonstrates that sin is so serious It requires death — and that God is so loving He took that death upon Himself for our sake.

Worship, then, is both reverent and rejoicing. We stand in awe of God's justice and mercy. The reality of the second death deepens our gratitude for the cross, humbles us before the majesty of God, and moves us to cry, *"Worthy is the Lamb who was slain!"* (Revelation 5:12). The believer's worship is not shallow sentiment, but informed awe — the kind that knows what we have been saved from.

Our eternal hope is not merely an escape from judgment but communion with God. As Revelation 21 reminds us, *"He will wipe every tear from their eyes. There will be no more death or mourning or crying or pain."* (v. 4). Why? Because the old order — including the second death — will have passed away. God is making all things new. The lake of fire will never touch the saints of God, not because we are worthy, but because Christ is worthy, and our names are written in His book.

Living in light of eternity

Finally, the doctrine of the second death should profoundly shape how we live. We are a people of eternity. We are citizens of heaven, not just participants in earthly routines. The awareness that eternity hangs in the balance for every person should lead to lives marked by compassion, boldness, and holy fear. We must not trivialize sin, for it is sin that leads to the second death. We must not grow numb to the lostness of those around us, for they too face an eternal future apart from Christ unless they repent and believe. And we must not forget the staggering grace that has rescued us — that our destiny was once the second death, but now it is eternal life in the presence of God.

As Paul exhorts in Philippians 2:12, we are to *"work out [our] salvation with fear and trembling."* Not because we doubt our security, but because we grasp the majesty and holiness of the God who has saved us. The doctrine of the second death is not designed to paralyze the believer, but to mobilize us to live holy, missional lives in joyful gratitude.

Every moment matters. Every conversation can carry eternal weight. Every act of love, every prayer for the lost, every word of gospel witness is part of God's plan to rescue people from the second death and bring them into eternal life.

13. SHEOL, HADES AND GEHENNA

Ancient words, eternal realities

When discussing death and the afterlife, the Bible employs a range of terms — Sheol, Hades, and Gehenna being the most prominent among them. These words are not mere synonyms; each carries a unique cultural, linguistic, and theological weight. Properly understanding these terms is essential for constructing a faithful Christian theology of death and judgment.

Words matter, and the vocabulary Scripture uses to speak of life beyond the grave is rich and deliberate. It reveals how ancient believers thought about death, how Jesus redefined and clarified those concepts, and how the Church should understand the ultimate destiny of humanity.

In this chapter, we aim to carefully examine the development and usage of these three key terms across the biblical narrative. We will not only explore their lexical meanings but also trace their theological trajectories — how these terms function within the story of redemption, culminating in the person and work of Christ. We begin with Sheol, the Hebrew term that dominates the Old Testament's discussion of the afterlife.

Sheol: The shadowy realm of the dead

In the Hebrew Bible, the term Sheol appears more than sixty times. It is the most common word used to describe the abode of the dead.

Unlike later Christian notions of heaven and hell, Sheol is not a place of reward or punishment. It is simply the grave, the underworld — the destination of all people, righteous and unrighteous alike. In Sheol, the dead dwell in a shadowy, silent, and unconscious state, cut off from the land of the living.

In Genesis 37:35, when Jacob believes his son Joseph is dead, he says, *"I will continue to mourn until I join my son in the grave (Sheol)."* Similarly, Job cries out, *"If only you would hide me in Sheol and conceal me till your anger has passed!"* (Job 14:13).

The psalmist speaks of being rescued from Sheol as deliverance from death itself: *"You, Lord, brought me up from the realm of the dead; you spared me from going down to the pit."* (Psalm 30:3). This language reflects an ancient, pre-resurrection understanding of death. In the Old Testament worldview, death was not the gateway to immediate reward or punishment but a descent into a murky, ambiguous existence. It was a place of no praise, no work, no remembrance — only waiting.

Psalm 88:10-12 poignantly asks: *"Do you show your wonders to the dead? Do their spirits rise up and praise you? Is your love declared in the grave, your faithfulness in Destruction? Are your wonders known in the place of darkness, or your righteous deeds in the land of oblivion?"*

Here, Sheol is depicted as a realm of forgetfulness and loss, not one of torment or peace. This understanding sets the stage for the later development of more differentiated afterlife concepts in Second Temple Judaism and the New Testament.

Importantly, Sheol was not considered hell in the modern sense. It was simply where all the dead went. Righteous figures like Jacob, David, and Job expected to go there. This indicates a theological tension: how could those in covenant with God share the same fate as the wicked? This tension would eventually be resolved in the progressive revelation of God's purposes — particularly through resurrection hope.

The development of resurrection hope

While early Israelite theology did not conceive of a detailed afterlife, later biblical texts begin to hint at something beyond Sheol. Daniel 12:2 is a pivotal verse: *"Multitudes who sleep in the dust of the earth will awake: some to everlasting life, others to shame and everlasting contempt."* This is one of the clearest Old Testament statements of bodily resurrection and a bifurcation of destinies — a radical development from the monolithic view of Sheol. Likewise, Isaiah 26:19 declares, *"But your dead will live, Lord; their bodies will rise — let those who dwell in the dust wake up and shout for joy."*

The shadows of Sheol are pierced by prophetic glimpses of restoration and life. Though these passages are few, they represent a major theological shift. Death is no longer the end of the story; the grave is no longer the final word. By the time of Jesus, Jewish beliefs about the afterlife had diversified. The Pharisees affirmed the resurrection of the dead and the existence of angels and spirits (Acts 23:8), while the Sadducees denied these things.

This diversity was rooted in the development of ideas that moved beyond the early Hebrew conception of Sheol as a single destination for all. In this evolving context, new terminology emerged — especially Hades and Gehenna — which clarified and extended the meaning of death, judgment, and the afterlife.

Hades: The Greek equivalent of Sheol

In the Greek translation of the Old Testament (the Septuagint), the word Hades was used to translate Sheol. Like Sheol, Hades referred broadly to the realm of the dead. However, by the New Testament period, Hades began to take on more nuance. It was sometimes used to refer to a temporary place of punishment or waiting, distinct from the final judgment associated with hell.

Jesus uses the term Hades in Luke 16:23 in the parable of the rich man and Lazarus: *"In Hades, where he was in torment, he looked up and saw Abraham far away, with Lazarus by his side."* Here we encounter a more developed view of the afterlife. The rich man is conscious, in torment, and separated from the comfort that Lazarus enjoys. Though some view this parable as metaphorical, it reveals the beliefs of the time: Hades was not a neutral place for all the dead, but a realm divided — with some in comfort and others in anguish.

Similarly, Jesus says to Peter in Matthew 16:18, *"I will build my church, and the gates of Hades will not overcome it."* This affirms that death itself will not triumph over the church — Hades will not hold God's people captive. In Revelation 1:18, the risen Christ declares, *"I hold the keys of death and Hades."*

This imagery presents Hades as a realm Christ has authority over — and from which He can release the dead. Thus, in the New Testament, Hades becomes not just the grave but a place of waiting — with implications of separation and judgment. It is the temporary holding place for the dead prior to final judgment, to be distinguished from the eternal destination described by another term: Gehenna.

Gehenna: From burning rubbish to final judgment

While Sheol and Hades refer primarily to the general realm of the dead or the intermediate state, Gehenna marks a distinct shift toward the concept of final judgment and eternal punishment. This term, unique to the New Testament, is not a Greek equivalent of Sheol but a theological development based on a real geographical location with a sordid history.

Gehenna is a transliteration of the Hebrew *Gē Hinnom* — which is the Valley of Hinnom — a ravine just south of Jerusalem. In Old Testament times, this valley became associated with the detestable practices of child sacrifice, particularly during the reigns of kings like Ahaz and Manasseh. Jeremiah condemns the people for burning their sons and daughters in fire, saying, *"They built high places for Baal in the Valley of Ben Hinnom to sacrifice their sons and daughters to Molek."* (Jeremiah 19:5).

Because of these abominations, the Valley of Hinnom became a symbol of divine judgment and was eventually cursed. By the time of Jesus, this valley had become a garbage dump where refuse and sometimes dead bodies were burned — a place of unending fire, stench, and decay. The fires of Gehenna became a vivid image in Jewish apocalyptic thought for the final judgment of the wicked.

Jesus uses Gehenna more than any other figure in the New Testament — always in the context of divine judgment. He warns in Matthew 5:22, *"Anyone who says, 'You fool!' will be in danger of the fire of hell (Gehenna)."* Again, in Matthew 10:28: *"Do not be afraid of those who kill the body but cannot kill the soul. Rather, be afraid of the One who can destroy both soul and body in hell (Gehenna)."*

The language Is stark, and it is intended to be. Gehenna is not a place of temporary waiting like Hades. It is the final destination for those who reject God — a place of irreversible judgment. The imagery Jesus uses includes *"unquenchable fire"* (Mark 9:43), *"outer darkness"* (Matthew 8:12), and *"weeping and gnashing of teeth"* (Matthew 13:42). These phrases are meant to arrest the hearer's attention and awaken a holy fear of the consequences of sin.

Gehenna and the nature of judgment

The use of Gehenna raises a deeper theological question: is this language literal or metaphorical? Is Jesus describing a literal lake of fire, or is He employing vivid imagery to convey a reality that transcends human comprehension?

Throughout church history, theologians have debated the nature of eternal punishment. Some have emphasized the literal flames and physical torment of hell, while others have interpreted the fire metaphorically, suggesting it symbolizes the anguish of separation from God, shame, or existential despair.

C.S. Lewis, for example, portrayed hell as self-imposed exile — the final outcome of a life spent rejecting God's invitation to grace.

Regardless of whether one interprets the fire as literal or symbolic, the weight of Scripture affirms the terrifying reality of Gehenna. Jesus consistently spoke of it as a place to be avoided at all costs. He urged drastic measures: *"If your right eye causes you to stumble, gouge it out... It is better for you to lose one part of your body than for your whole body to be thrown into hell* (Gehenna).*"* (Matthew 5:29). This is not hyperbole for rhetorical flair — it is a serious warning from the Lord of life.

Gehenna, then, is the final and eternal expression of divine justice. It is not merely the natural consequence of human rebellion; it is the righteous judgment of a holy God against all evil. Unlike Sheol or Hades, which are temporary and will one day be emptied (Revelation 20:13-14), Gehenna is permanent.

Revelation describes the final judgment this way: *"Then death and Hades were thrown into the lake of fire. The lake of fire is the second death"* (Revelation 20:14). This *"lake of fire"* is the culmination of the imagery of Gehenna — the place where evil is decisively and eternally dealt with.

Jesus and the redefinition of death's realms

What makes the teachings Jesus' so revolutionary is how He reorients all three of these terms — Sheol, Hades, and Gehenna — around Himself. He does not simply affirm traditional Jewish beliefs about death; He redefines and fulfils them.

First, Jesus proclaims victory over Hades. *"I was dead, and now look, I am alive for ever and ever! And I hold the keys of death and Hades."* (Revelation 1:18). Christ is not merely a teacher of the afterlife — He is the Lord of it. He has entered into death and emerged victorious, holding the keys of the grave. This is not poetic language; it is a declaration of supreme authority.

Second, Jesus promises deliverance from Sheol. Where the psalmist cried out from the realm of the dead, Jesus descended into it and overcame it. The resurrection is not merely the rescue of one man from death; it is the decisive defeat of Sheol's power. As Peter proclaims in his Pentecost sermon, quoting Psalm 16, *"You will not abandon me to the realm of the dead, you will not let your holy one see decay."* (Acts 2:27). This resurrection promise now extends to all who are united with Christ.

Third, Jesus warns of Gehenna not as a relic of Old Testament judgment, but as a present and future reality for those who reject the Kingdom. The way of Jesus is not merely an invitation to abundant life; it is also a call to flee from wrath. The narrow path that leads to life must be walked intentionally, for the broad path leads to destruction (Matthew 7:13-14). Thus, Christ does not merely use these terms — He actually fulfils them. He transforms Sheol from a place of silence into a place of hope. He takes the keys of Hades and opens the door to resurrection. And He warns us of Gehenna, not to frighten us into legalism, but to awaken us to the gravity of our choices and the holiness of God.

From Hebrew shadows to Christian clarity

Understanding Sheol, Hades, and Gehenna provides more than just a linguistic or historical study. These terms illuminate the theological development of biblical views on death, judgment, and the afterlife. They trace a trajectory from the dim shadows of the Old Testament to the blazing clarity of Christ's resurrection. And in that arc, we see God's progressive revelation of His justice, mercy, and ultimate purposes for humanity.

From fear to fulfilment

In the Old Testament, Sheol is shrouded in great mystery — a shadowy place beneath the earth, where both the righteous and the wicked go. It evokes fear, silence, and distance from God. This fear of the unknown often led to a strong longing for God's presence even in death. The Psalmist cries out, *"Among the dead no one proclaims your name. Who praises you from the grave?"* (6:5). But the resurrection of Jesus changes everything. The fear that once defined Sheol is transformed by the bright hope of eternal life.

No longer do the righteous face a silent, shadowy end. Instead, they anticipate being *"at home with the Lord."* (2 Corinthians 5:8). The grave has lost its sting, and death has been swallowed up in victory (1 Corinthians 15:54-55). What was once a descent into silence has become a transition into glory.

This fulfilment is not a contradiction of Old Testament hope but its culmination. The saints of Israel believed that God would not ultimately abandon them to the grave. That hope now finds its anchor in the risen Christ. As Jesus declares, *"I am the resurrection and the life. The one who believes in me will live, even though they die"* (John 11:25). The former fear of Sheol gives way to faith in the One who conquered it.

The interim and the eternal

The development of Hades and Gehenna in the New Testament reveals a vital distinction between two aspects of the afterlife: the intermediate state and the final judgment.

Hades represents the temporary holding place for the dead — particularly the wicked — while they await the final judgment. In Luke 16, Jesus presents a parable of a rich man and Lazarus, where the rich man is in torment in Hades, and Lazarus is comforted in *"Abraham's side."* This illustrates an interim state where the destinies of the dead are already differentiated, even before the final resurrection and judgment.

However, Hades is not permanent. Revelation 20:13-14 affirms that death and Hades will be thrown into the lake of fire. This means that even the realm of the dead will itself be judged and abolished. The temporal nature of Hades emphasizes that God's purposes are not complete until all is brought into account before His throne.

Gehenna, in contrast, represents the eternal outcome of that judgment — the final and irrevocable separation from God. Jesus warns repeatedly of Gehenna as a place to be avoided at all costs. It is not purgative, reformative, or temporary. It is the end for those who reject the grace of God and persist in rebellion. The eternal fire, the undying worm, and the outer darkness are all symbols pointing to the horror of ultimate exile from the presence of God (cf. Matthew 25:41, Mark 9:48).

This distinction helps us avoid theological confusion. The righteous dead are with Christ now, awaiting resurrection glory. The unrighteous dead are held in Hades, awaiting final sentencing. But Gehenna is the final place of punishment — not Hades. This clarity is crucial for understanding both the justice and mercy of God in dealing with sin.

Implications for Christian theology and discipleship

These terms are not relics of ancient cosmology. They are enduring theological concepts that shape how we understand the seriousness of sin, the urgency of salvation, and the depth of Christ's work on our behalf. First, these biblical terms confront us with the reality of divine judgment. In a culture that prefers comfort to conviction, Jesus' stark references to Gehenna are jarring. Yet He speaks of it more than anyone else. Why?

Because the love of God is not sentimental; it is holy. A holy God must judge sin. Hell is not the absence of God's love, but the manifestation of His justice. It is what happens when people reject the only cure for sin — the mercy of Christ.

Second, these terms highlight the necessity of the cross. If sin did not carry eternal consequences, then the cross of Christ would be unnecessary. But Jesus bore our sin and endured divine wrath precisely because Gehenna is real. The gospel is not simply a path to a better life — it is rescue from eternal destruction. As Paul writes, *"He delivered us from the domain of darkness and brought us into the kingdom of the Son he loves."* (Colossians 1:13).

Third, these truths fuel evangelistic urgency. If Hades is real — a place of conscious separation from God — and Gehenna is worse — a place of final judgment — then we cannot be passive about the gospel. We must be proclaiming the good news with urgency, compassion, and boldness. The stakes could not be higher.

Finally, these teachings offer comfort for the believer. In Christ, we no longer fear Sheol or Hades. We are secure in Him. As Paul confidently says in Philippians 1:21, *"To live is Christ and to die is gain."* Death becomes a doorway, not a dungeon. The Christian hope is not just life after death — it is resurrection after death, and everlasting joy in the presence of God.

A unified vision of death and judgment

By tracing the trajectory from Sheol to Hades to Gehenna, we discover a coherent theological framework. The Bible does not present a chaotic or contradictory view of the afterlife. Rather, it offers a progressive revelation that finds its climax in Jesus Christ.

- Sheol teaches us the inevitability and mystery of death.
- Hades teaches us the accountability and interim consequences of our choices.
- Gehenna teaches us the finality and severity of divine judgment.

And in every case, Christ is central. He is the one who descended to the realm of the dead and rose again (Ephesians 4:9-10). He is the Judge who warns of Gehenna, yet also the Saviour who bore its judgment in our place. He is the King who will one day throw death and Hades into the lake of fire, making all things new (Revelation 21:1-5).

Thus, Christian theology is not fixated on death, but on resurrection. We study Sheol, Hades, and Gehenna not to foster fear, but to deepen faith — to understand what we've been saved from and what we've been saved for. Our hope is not in escaping punishment, but in embracing a Person: the risen Jesus, who holds the keys of death and Hades and who opens the door to eternal life.

As we contemplate these terms, let us not be morbid or speculative. Let us be very grateful. Grateful that the silence of Sheol is broken by the voice of the Shepherd. Grateful that the chains of Hades are shattered by the One who descended into the grave. And grateful that the fires of Gehenna need not touch us — for the wrath of God was poured out on the Lamb, who takes away the sin of the world.

14. THE DEATH OF DEATH IN THE DEATH OF CHRIST

Throughout the Bible, death looms as the greatest enemy of humanity, a dark shadow over every life, the inevitable end of every journey. Yet the New Testament does not just announce victory over death—it declares the death of death itself. And this radical triumph comes not through denial, avoidance, or human strength, but through the suffering and death of Christ. The irony of the gospel is this: death is defeated by death—specifically, the death of the sinless Son of God.

No text captures this more powerfully than Paul's declaration In Romans 6: *"For we know that since Christ was raised from the dead, he cannot die again; death no longer has mastery over him."* (6:9). The mastery of death is broken because Jesus has passed through it and emerged victorious. In doing so, He has secured for all who are united to Him a share in that victory. This chapter explores how union with Christ—particularly in His death and resurrection—marks the definitive end of death's reign.

United with Christ in death and resurrection

The doctrine of union with Christ lies at the heart of the New Testament's teaching on salvation. When Paul proclaims, *"I have been crucified with Christ and I no longer live, but Christ lives in me."* (Galatians 2:20), he is not speaking in metaphor alone. He is describing a real spiritual participation in the death and life of Jesus. This is not merely moral inspiration or symbolic identification. It is a mystical, Spirit-enabled bond that joins believers to the historical events of Christ's crucifixion and resurrection.

Nowhere is this more explicitly stated than in Romans 6:3-5: *"Don't you know that all of us who were baptized into Christ Jesus were baptized into his death? We were therefore buried with him through baptism into death in order that, just as Christ was raised from the dead through the glory of the Father, we too may live a new life. For if we have been united with him in a death like his, we will certainly also be united with him in a resurrection like his."*

This union has two aspects: death and life. The first is radical and sobering—when Christ died, the believer died with Him. That is, the old self, enslaved to sin and subject to judgment, was put to death in Christ. This is not a gradual moral improvement but a decisive act of divine judgment, executed on Calvary. The believer is no longer *"in Adam,"* under the reign of sin and death, but *"in Christ,"* where life and grace rule.

The second aspect is equally transformative — resurrection. Because believers share in Christ's death, they also share in His life, and this is not merely future hope; it is present reality. Paul says in Romans 6:8, *"Now if we died with Christ, we believe that we will also live with him."* This new life begins now, though it will be consummated in the resurrection of the body.

The death of Christ, therefore, is not merely substitutionary—it is participatory. He dies for us, but we also die with Him. His resurrection is not merely proof of victory—it is the source of our victory. In union with Christ, we are pulled through death into life.

Death as a dethroned tyrant

The apostle Paul speaks of death not simply as a biological event, but as a power. Death reigns (Romans 5:17), death has a sting (1 Corinthians 15:56), and it exercises dominion over all creation. It is the final enemy (1 Corinthians 15:26), the last tyrant to be destroyed. And in the ancient world, tyrants did not relinquish power willingly. They had to be overthrown.

This is precisely what Christ's death accomplished. On the cross, Jesus disarmed the rulers and authorities, triumphing over them (Colossians 2:15). Chief among these defeated powers is death itself. The resurrection is not merely a reversal of death—it is a public declaration of death's defeat.

This is why Paul can speak in celebratory tones at the conclusion of 1 Corinthians 15: *"Where, O death, is your victory? Where, O death, is your sting? ... Thanks be to God! He gives us the victory through our Lord Jesus Christ."*

The question is rhetorical, even mocking. Death's victory is undone. Its sting—the result of sin—is removed. And how? Through the death of Jesus. It is not His miracles or moral teachings that dethrone death, but His cross. He does not conquer death by avoiding it, but by stepping into it and shattering it from the inside out. In this way, the Christian gospel turns the entire narrative of human mortality on its head. The place of greatest horror—Golgotha—becomes the site of cosmic victory. The instrument of torture—the cross—becomes the tree of life. The event of deepest despair—the death of the Son of God—becomes the death of death.

Atonement and the defeat of death

Why did Christ have to die? Theories of atonement throughout church history have emphasized different aspects: penal substitution, moral influence, Christus Victor, and more. But central to all is the recognition that Christ's death addresses the root problem of sin, which is inseparably linked to death. As Paul teaches, *"the wages of sin is death."* (Romans 6:23). To deal with sin is to deal with death—and vice versa.

In bearing sin on the cross, Jesus bore its ultimate consequence. His cry, *"My God, my God, why have you forsaken me?"* reflects the alienation sin brings. But in doing so, He breaks the link between sin and death for those who believe. *"He died to sin once for all,"* Paul says (Romans 6:10), and in doing so, He broke the power that sin held through death. This is why the death of Christ is not merely the end of one man's life, but the end of death's reign. His death satisfies justice, absorbs wrath, breaks the curse, and opens the door to life. All these images converge at the cross. The One, who is Life, allows Himself to be killed, so that in dying, He might kill death.

Victory secured, life bestowed

Having seen that union with Christ brings believers into His death and resurrection, we now turn to the fuller implications of that victory—how the death of Christ not only nullifies death's power but grants new life to all who are in Him.

The cross is not a tragic necessity but a glorious conquest. And in that conquest, Christ has not merely rescued individuals from the grave but inaugurated a new creation.

The resurrection as the seal of victory

The resurrection of Jesus Christ is not merely the reversal of Good Friday's defeat; it is the public declaration that death has been decisively overthrown. Without the resurrection, the cross would remain a noble but failed protest against evil. With the resurrection, the cross becomes the instrument of cosmic victory.

Paul writes in Romans 4:25 that Jesus *"was delivered over to death for our sins and was raised to life for our justification."* The resurrection proves that the sacrifice was accepted, the debt paid, and sin's reign ended. And because death is the consequence of sin, when sin is dealt with, death no longer holds authority.

The New Testament repeatedly links Jesus' resurrection to the believer's hope. As Paul says in 1 Corinthians 15:20-22: *"But Christ has indeed been raised from the dead, the first fruits of those who have fallen asleep. For since death came through a man, the resurrection of the dead comes also through a man. For as in Adam all die, so in Christ all will be made alive."*

Christ is the first fruits—the guarantee of a greater harvest. Just as Adam brought death to all, so Christ brings life to all who are united to Him. The resurrection is not merely a past event; it is a future promise and a present power.

Eternal life begins now

One of the most radical aspects of New Testament teaching is that eternal life does not begin at death—it begins at conversion. The believer already has *"passed from death to life"* (John 5:24). Paul echoes this in Ephesians 2:4-6: *"But because of his great love for us, God, who is rich in mercy, made us alive with Christ even when we were dead in transgressions—it is by grace you have been saved. And God raised us up with Christ and seated us with him in the heavenly realms in Christ Jesus."*

This new life is not merely a future hope; it is a present reality. It transforms the believer's relationship to sin, death, and the world. Sin no longer reigns. Death no longer terrorizes. The grave no longer speaks the final word.

This is why Paul can say in Romans 8:11:"*And if the Spirit of him who raised Jesus from the dead is living in you, he who raised Christ from the dead will also give life to your mortal bodies because of his Spirit who lives in you.*" The indwelling Spirit is the evidence of resurrection power already at work. The same Spirit who raised Jesus will raise the believer—and is already animating new life within them.

Life through death

The paradox of Christian faith is this: to live, we must first die. Jesus taught this principle repeatedly. *"Whoever wants to save their life will lose it,"* He said, *"but whoever loses their life for me will find it."* (Matthew 16:25). The path to life runs through death.

This is true not only of Christ's redemptive work, but of the believer's daily walk. Paul declares in Corinthians 15:31, *"I die every day"* and again in 2 Corinthians 4:10, *"We always carry around in our body the death of Jesus, so that the life of Jesus may also be revealed in our body."* Death and life are intertwined. We die to sin, die to self, die to the world—so that Christ may live in us. This is not morbid but liberating. The death of death means that we no longer have to cling to the false securities of this world. We can surrender freely, love generously, serve sacrificially, and live courageously—because death has been defeated. *"To live is Christ and to die is gain"* (Philippians 1:21) is not a slogan—it is a worldview.

Freedom from the fear of death

The book of Hebrews adds another dimension to Christ's death: it liberates from fear. *"Since the children have flesh and blood,"* the author writes, *"he too shared in their humanity so that by his death he might break the power of him who holds the power of death — that is, the devil — and free those who all their lives were held in slavery by their fear of death."* (Hebrews 2:14–15).

Fear of death is a form of slavery. It distorts our desires, fuels our anxieties, and keeps us bound to the world. But in the death of Christ, that fear is dismantled. Not because death ceases to exist—but because its power is broken. It can no longer accuse, enslave, or destroy. It has become a doorway, not a dungeon. The fear of death is replaced with the hope of glory. The believer no longer dreads the end of life but anticipates the fullness of it.

As Paul writes in 2 Corinthians 5:1: *"For we know that if the earthly tent we live in is destroyed, we have a building from God, an eternal house in heaven, not built by human hands."* This confidence changes everything. It reshapes grief, reframes suffering, and reorients priorities. It frees the Christian to live with open hands and courageous hearts.

The triumph of the Lamb

The final scenes of Scripture depict the complete and final defeat of death. In Revelation 20:14, we read that *"death and Hades were thrown into the lake of fire. The lake of fire is the second death."* Then in Revelation 21:4, the glorious promise: *"There will be no more death or mourning or crying or pain, for the old order of things has passed away."*

Death dies. The last enemy is destroyed. And who brings this to pass? The Lamb who was slain. The victory is not won by brute force, but by sacrificial love. As Revelation 5 declares, *"Worthy is the Lamb, who was slain, to receive power and wealth and wisdom and strength and honour and glory and praise!"* It is the crucified Christ who reigns. It is the One who laid down His life who receives the crown. The cross is not the prelude to glory; it is the path to it. And through that cross, death has been swallowed up in victory.

Living the reality of death's defeat

To understand that death has been defeated is one thing; to live as if that victory is true is another. The gospel declares that the death of Christ has rendered death powerless, but the ongoing call to the Church is to embody that reality in a world still gripped by fear, decay, and mortality.

The resurrection life of Jesus Is not only future promise; It is present power to live unshackled from death's dominion.

Living as people of the resurrection

In Romans 6, Paul outlines the practical implications of union with Christ: *"In the same way, count yourselves dead to sin but alive to God in Christ Jesus. Therefore, do not let sin reign in your mortal body so that you obey its evil desires."* (Romans 6:11-12).

Believers are to reckon themselves dead to the old order and alive to the new. This reckoning is not mental gymnastics but spiritual realism. We are to live in the power of the resurrection now — not waiting for the grave to experience new life but embodying it in the present.

This resurrection life is marked by freedom: freedom from sin, from fear, from condemnation. Paul continues in the book of Romans with the triumphant declaration: *"Therefore, there is now no condemnation for those who are in Christ Jesus, because through Christ Jesus the law of the Spirit who gives life has set you free from the law of sin and death."* (Romans 8:1-2).

The law of sin and death once reigned over us like a tyrant. But now a greater power is at work: the Spirit who gives life. This new law has set us free, not by ignoring sin, but by dealing with it fully in the death of Christ. We are no longer slaves. We are no longer bound by the fear of death. We are children of the resurrection.

Worship in the shadow of the cross

Christian worship is always shadowed by the cross and illumined by the empty tomb. Every Lord's Supper, every baptism, every funeral, every hymn of praise finds its meaning in the death that brought life. We worship a crucified and risen Lord.

This paradox is central to Christian identity. We proclaim *"Christ crucified"* – a scandal and a mystery to the world, but the wisdom and power of God to those being saved.

In the cross, we see the justice of God satisfied and the mercy of God magnified. In the resurrection, we see the validation of the Son and the promise of our future.

This shapes our worship. It becomes not just a time of emotional uplift, but a defiant proclamation: death has no power here. Every time the Church gathers, it rehearses the victory of the Lamb and declares the end of the grave's dominion. The songs of the saints are battle hymns against the darkness.

Pastoral courage in the face of death

The knowledge that death has been defeated in Christ equips pastors and believers to minister in moments of deepest grief. When death enters the lives of our people—through loss, diagnosis, aging, or despair—we do not offer platitudes or distractions. We offer a Person. We proclaim that the One who died now lives and reigns.

This enables Christians to mourn with hope, to grieve without despair, and to face the dying process without terror. The presence of Christ in suffering is not theoretical—it is incarnational. He knows our weakness. He shared our sorrows. He tasted death, so that when we face it, we do so not alone but with Him.

And He is not only beside us; He has gone before us. As Hebrews says, Jesus has entered the inner sanctuary *"as a forerunner on our behalf."* (6:20). He has blazed a trail through death into glory. His presence transforms hospice rooms into holy ground. His promises light the shadows of every valley of death.

A mission fuelled by resurrection power

If death has died, then the Church must rise. The mission of God's people is not simply to comfort the grieving but to proclaim the death of death to a dying world. We preach not a message of mere moral reform or personal growth, but of cosmic renewal and eschatological hope. The defeat of death empowers bold evangelism.

If Jesus is Lord even over the grave, then there is no place too dark, no heart too hard, no loss too deep for His redeeming grace. Christians are heralds of resurrection in a culture obsessed with decay. We speak life where the world accepts death as inevitable. And we suffer with purpose.

Paul writes in 2 Corinthians 4:16-17: *"Therefore we do not lose heart. Though outwardly we are wasting away, yet inwardly we are being renewed day by day. For our light and momentary troubles are achieving for us an eternal glory that far outweighs them all."*

Even as our bodies age and our pain increases, we see beyond the veil. Death no longer mocks us — it works for us. It becomes, paradoxically, the servant of glory. The very afflictions that once signalled our end now become instruments of transformation.

A church shaped by cruciform glory

To embrace the death of death is to become a cruciform people — shaped by the cross and radiant with resurrection. It means laying down pride, power, and self-preservation, and rising into humility, love, and courage. The Church of the risen Christ must live as if the tomb is empty.

This means we are not shocked by suffering. We do not panic in decline. We do not flinch in persecution. The world may appear to be falling apart, but we know the end of the story. And it ends not with a grave, but with a throne. The death of death also creates unity. All who are in Christ have died and risen with Him. Race, class, age, nationality — none of these distinctions define us anymore. We are one people, shaped by one death, raised by one life.

The final word belongs to the Lamb

As we look to the end, we return to Revelation. The Lamb stands at the centre of the throne, and the nations gather to worship Him — not because He conquered with the sword, but because He was slain. The final victory song is not about human greatness but divine grace.

"Then I saw a new heaven and a new earth… He will wipe every tear from their eyes. There will be no more death" (Revelation 21:1, 4).

This is our hope. Not escape from death, but the destruction of it. Not denial of the grave, but its glorious defeat. The gospel does not offer mere comfort; it proclaims conquest. Death is dead. Christ is risen. The grave has lost its sting.

And because of that, we live—boldly, joyfully, sacrificially—knowing that we are forever united to the One who conquered death by dying.

15. GRIEF WITH HOPE: CHRISTIAN MOURNING

The tension between sorrow and assurance

In every generation, Christians have stood at gravesides with a peculiar mix of tears and hope. We mourn like anyone else, yet not like everyone else. The pain of loss still pierces our hearts, but our grief is infused with something deeper than sorrow — an unshakable confidence in resurrection. This paradox is at the heart of Christian mourning. We are people who grieve, but not as those who have no hope (1 Thessalonians 4:13).

The human reality of grief

Grief is not an indication of spiritual weakness or theological ignorance. It is a normal, human response to the rupture that death brings. When Jesus approached the tomb of Lazarus, even knowing He would raise him, He wept (John 11:35). His tears were not staged or strategic — they were real. The Son of God, perfect in holiness and truth, was moved by the grief of those He loved.

In this moment, Jesus validates our mourning. He does not scold Mary and Martha for their sorrow. He joins it. His presence there affirms that sorrow is not sinful. It is sacred. To mourn is to love and love always aches in the face of loss. Christian faith does not silence sorrow; it sanctifies it.

When Paul exhorts the Thessalonians not to grieve *"like the rest of mankind, who have no hope,"* he is not commanding joy in the face of tragedy. He is distinguishing Christian grief from hopeless grief — not opposing grief altogether. The grief of the believer is real but redemptive. It flows from love and looks toward resurrection.

The community of the grieving

The body of Christ is never more needed than in seasons of loss. Christian mourning is not a solitary experience; it is shared within the fellowship of the Church. That's why Paul writes, *"Mourn with those who mourn."* (Romans 12:15)

This is not an optional virtue—it is a command rooted in the solidarity of the gospel. In Galatians 6:2, we are called to *"carry each other's burdens,"* and nowhere is this more crucial than in grief. Funerals, memorials, vigils, meals—these are sacred acts of burden-bearing. The Christian community surrounds the grieving, not simply with answers, but with presence. Often, the ministry of silent companionship speaks more loudly than any sermon.

Job's friends provide a cautionary tale. When they sat in silence with him for seven days, they ministered well. It was only when they began to speak, trying to explain or justify his suffering, that they erred. In times of mourning, theological correctness can sometimes obscure pastoral wisdom. The best comforters often say least and stay longest.

The community of believers embodies the comfort of Christ. When someone brings food, weeps beside us, writes a note, or simply listens, the hands and heart of Jesus are made tangible. Mourning with hope does not remove pain; it surrounds it with love.

Hope grounded in resurrection

What separates Christian mourning from worldly sorrow is not a lack of sadness, but a deep and abiding confidence in the resurrection of the dead. Paul's pastoral words to the Thessalonians are anchored in the promise that *"we believe that Jesus died and rose again, and so we believe that God will bring with Jesus those who have fallen asleep in him."* (1 Thessalonians 4:14).

Our hope is not sentimental; it is historical. It is rooted in an empty tomb and confirmed by hundreds of witnesses. The resurrection of Jesus is not only a theological doctrine—it is a cosmic declaration: death does not have the final word. Because Christ is risen, those who die in Him will also rise. This changes everything. We do not say goodbye to our loved ones forever, but only for a time. The separation is real, but not final. The grave is not a wall; It Is a doorway. This conviction transforms grief. It does not erase it, but it reframes it.

This hope does not dull the ache, but it gives it meaning. Our sorrow becomes longing. Our tears become prayers. Our mourning becomes waiting—watchful, hopeful, expectant. We ache for the reunion that is promised. And that longing is not foolish optimism; it is faith fixed on a Person who has conquered death.

The tension we must embrace

Living in the *"already and not yet"* of resurrection hope means living with tension. We believe in victory over death, but we still feel its sting. We confess eternal life, but we still bury those we love. This paradox can be disorienting, even discouraging, if not properly understood. It is vital to resist the temptation to rush through grief with spiritual slogans. Common phrases like *"They're in a better place"* or *"God needed another angel"* may be well-intentioned, but they often bypass the depth of pain. Biblical hope does not demand a quick recovery. It grants permission to lament. The Psalms are full of sorrow and many questions, showing that honest mourning is part of godly faith.

Christian hope is not fragile. It does not require denial or emotional suppression. It is robust enough to withstand the storms of loss. It invites us to cry, to question, to groan—and still to believe. In fact, groaning is a mark of hope. Paul says in Romans 8:23, *"We ourselves, who have the first fruits of the Spirit, groan inwardly as we wait eagerly for our adoption, the redemption of our bodies."* Groaning is not weakness; it is longing. It is the soul's cry for what is not yet, rooted in what already is. This is the tension of Christian mourning: we weep, but not without hope; we groan, but not in despair.

Consolation, worship, and the witness of hope

Grief with hope is not merely a private comfort; it becomes a public testimony. The way Christians mourn sends a message to the world. When we sorrow deeply and yet cling fiercely to the promises of God, we bear witness to a kingdom not of this world.

Our grief does not silence our faith—it amplifies it.

The consolation of Christ

At the centre of our hope in mourning is a Person—not merely a doctrine or a destination. Jesus said, *"Blessed are those who mourn, for they will be comforted."* (Matthew 5:4). He did not say they will be distracted or numbed but comforted. This comfort is not the removal of grief, but the presence of God within it.

The consolation Christ offers is both present and future. In this life, we are comforted by His Spirit—our *"Counsellor,"* our *"Comforter,"* who dwells within us. He is the One who reminds us of the truth when our hearts falter, who intercedes with groans when we cannot pray, who strengthens us to endure when sorrow overwhelms. And yet, even this consolation points forward. Revelation 21:4 speaks of the day when *"He will wipe every tear from their eyes. There will be no more death or mourning or crying or pain."* This is not a metaphor—it is a promise. God Himself will dry every tear. The hands that were pierced for our redemption will touch the faces of the redeemed.

The comfort of Christ is both now and not yet. In our mourning, we experience glimpses of it—quiet moments of peace, sudden clarity in Scripture, the support of a friend. But we await its fullness. Grief in the Christian life is always pregnant with hope, always straining toward the Day when death is swallowed up in victory.

Worship in the midst of grief

Christian mourning is not silent. It may begin in groaning, but it often ends in praise. The Psalms are filled with examples of this trajectory: the psalmist cries out in agony, pours out complaint, wrestles with despair—but then, somehow, finds his way to worship. This is not a denial of grief; it is its sanctification. Worship in sorrow is one of the most powerful acts of faith.

It declares that God is still good, even when life is not. It affirms that He is still worthy, even when our hearts are broken. It is the language of the soul that chooses trust, even when it does not feel triumphant.

Job, in the ashes of his loss, fell to the ground in worship and said, *"The Lord gave and the Lord has taken away; may the name of the Lord be praised."* (Job 1:21). His words were not stoic, nor were they simplistic. They were a profound expression of reverence in the presence of mystery.

Worship does not require understanding. It does not resolve every question. But it orients us toward God. It reminds us who He is and who we are in Him. It lifts our eyes from the grave to the throne. In mourning, worship becomes an act of defiance against despair and a declaration of allegiance to hope.

The witness of hope

One of the most powerful testimonies a Christian can give is how they respond to death. In a world that either denies death or despairs because of it, the believer stands out. Not because we do not cry, but because we do not collapse. Not because we have no pain, but because we have a Person who walks with us through it.

When Paul wrote to the Thessalonians about grieving with hope, he framed it in the context of encouragement and witness. After describing the return of Christ and the resurrection of the dead, he wrote, *"Therefore encourage one another with these words."* (1 Thessalonians 4:18). Our eschatology—the truths of what lies ahead—is not merely for doctrine, but for encouragement and evangelism.

Funerals, in particular, become gospel opportunities. The reality of death opens hearts to eternal questions. When the Church surrounds the grieving with presence and praise, with Scripture and silence, it shows a better way to die—and to live. Christian funerals are not mere ceremonies; they are proclamations. They tell the truth about death, but also about life, love, hope, and resurrection. The contrast is striking. Where the world clings to memory, the Christian clings to promise. Where others speak only of legacy, we speak of reunion. Where others close the book, we turn the page. The Christian witness in mourning is not a denial of death's sorrow—it is a declaration of death's defeat.

Living in the light of our hope

Mourning is not only about remembering the dead; it is about how we live in the light of what we believe. The hope we carry into grief is the same hope we carry into every day. It shapes how we view aging, sickness, suffering, and loss. It informs our values and priorities. It urges us to treasure each day as a gift and to live with eternity in view.

This hope should make us more compassionate, more patient, more courageous. It should loosen our grip on this world without detaching us from its beauty and responsibilities. We mourn because we love — and we hope because we believe.

To live with Christian hope is not to live in denial, but in defiance. We defy despair, we resist the lie that death is the end, and we proclaim that a greater reality is coming. The risen Christ has gone ahead of us, and one day He will return. Until then, we mourn with hope. We grieve with trust. And we wait — not in fear, but in faith.

16. DYING WELL: BEING PREPARED

Throughout history, Christians have been known not only for how they lived but also for how they died. In a world that often shuns the thought of death, believers are called to prepare for it — not with fear, but with faith; not with dread, but with dignity.

To die well is not to welcome death, but to face it in the fullness of gospel hope, trusting in Christ, and leaving behind a witness that brings comfort to others and glory to God. This preparation involves the heart, the home, and the Church, each shaped by the promise of life beyond the grave.

Preparing the heart: embracing the reality of mortality

It is sobering to realise that unless Christ returns in our lifetime, every single one of us will face death. Yet this is not a thought to be avoided — it is a truth to be redeemed. Scripture reminds us of this reality: *"Teach us to number our days, that we may gain a heart of wisdom."* (Psalm 90:12). Wisdom begins when we accept the brevity of life and live accordingly.

Preparing our hearts begins with acknowledging our mortality. The modern world cultivates denial, hiding death behind hospital curtains and polished funeral services. But Christians are called to live in the light of eternity. Paul declares, *"For to me, to live is Christ and to die is gain."* (Philippians 1:21). This radical statement is only possible when one's heart is anchored in the gospel. Death is not a tragic end but a departure to be with Christ, which Paul describes as *"better by far"* (Philippians 1:23).

The believer prepares to die well by cultivating a life of ongoing repentance, worship, and trust. We do not wait until the shadow of death falls to turn our hearts to heaven. Daily disciplines of prayer, Scripture meditation, and obedience to Christ help shape a readiness that does not panic when the end nears. Jesus said, *"Do not let your hearts be troubled. You believe in God; believe also in me."* (John 14:1). He prepares a place for us — and we must prepare our hearts for that place.

Reckoning with unfinished business

Dying well also involves resolving the unresolved. Many people carry the weight of broken relationships, unconfessed sin, or deferred obedience. As death approaches, these burdens become heavier. But we do not need to wait until the final weeks of life to pursue reconciliation.

Jesus urged His disciples to be proactive in making peace: *"Settle matters quickly with your adversary* (Matthew 5:25). Paul commands, *"If it is possible, as far as it depends on you, live at peace with everyone."* (Romans 12:18).

Living in peace with others is part of dying well. Forgiveness extended or received, words of love spoken, apologies offered — these are the acts that prepare the soul for departure. As we reflect on our relationships, let us ask whether there is someone we need to reach out to, someone who needs to hear the gospel or be reminded of our love.

Ordering the inner life

Our readiness for death also touches the ordering of our inner life — our affections, values, and hopes. The writer of Ecclesiastes observes, *"It is better to go to a house of mourning than to go to a house of feasting, for death is the destiny of everyone; the living should take this to heart."* (Ecclesiastes 7:2). There is wisdom in contemplating death, for it clarifies what truly matters.

When our lives are ruled by temporal priorities, death is a thief. But when we live for the eternal, death becomes a doorway. Jesus said, *"Where your treasure is, there your heart will be also."* (Matthew 6:21). To die well is to have one's treasure — and thus one's heart — in heaven.

This perspective compels us to loosen our grip on possessions and status and to fix our eyes on what lies ahead. Paul encourages believers to *"set your hearts on things above, where Christ is."* (Colossians 3:1). Preparing to die well is not just about the end of life — it is about how we live every day in view of eternity.

The witness of a well-prepared life

In a world that denies death or treats it as taboo, Christians who prepare for death in peace and trust provide a countercultural witness. A believer whose life testifies to faith, love, and hope — right up to their final breath — becomes a living sermon. Paul modelled this with confidence when he wrote, *"I have fought the good fight, I have finished the race, I have kept the faith. Now there is in store for me the crown of righteousness."* (2 Timothy 4:7–8). Such confidence does not arise spontaneously at death's door; it is cultivated over time in a life anchored in Christ.

Preparing to die well means learning to live well, grounded in spiritual disciplines that foster intimacy with God. Regular prayer, the reading of Scripture, participation in the sacraments, and fellowship in the church shape our hearts and train us to entrust every season — including our last — to God. Spiritual maturity does not immunize us from suffering, but it teaches us to suffer redemptively. It is not stoicism that marks the Christian dying well, but serenity that flows from a known and trusted Shepherd.

When believers live and die with such courage and clarity, their families are often deeply affected. Even non-believing loved ones take notice of the peace that attends a faithful death. The early Christians were known for their joyful funerals, marked by singing, thanksgiving, and the proclamation of resurrection. They grieved, yes — but they grieved with hope. The contrast to the fear-driven mourning of pagan culture was striking. Even today, the calm confidence of a dying Christian often opens hearts to the gospel in ways that years of apologetics never could.

Preparing our loved ones

A crucial element of dying well is preparing our families, not just practically but spiritually. While end-of-life documents such as wills, advance care directives, and funeral plans are important, they pale in comparison to the impact of a legacy of love and faith. The best inheritance a Christian can leave is a life that testifies to the goodness of God.

Conversations about death should not be postponed until illness forces the issue. Families benefit when aging parents or terminally ill members speak openly and biblically about what they believe, what they hope for, and what matters most to them. When such dialogue takes place early and often, it brings clarity, peace, and unity.

For example, a father who has lived for Christ and taught his children the Scriptures will often find that his last words echo long after he is gone. If he can say, with Paul, *"to live is Christ and to die is gain,"* then his family, while grieving, will rejoice in knowing where he is — and who he is with.

On the other hand, those who delay these conversations often leave their families in confusion or even conflict about medical decisions, burial choices, and spiritual matters.

Such lack of preparation can add unnecessary emotional distress to a time already marked by loss. Letters written to children or grandchildren, prayers recorded or written in journals, and Bibles filled with notes of wisdom and love become treasures that last generations. They remind loved ones that faith is not just a Sunday ritual but a living, breathing reality that touches every aspect of life — and death.

Discipling the church to embrace mortality

Churches, too, must take responsibility for helping believers prepare to die well. Sadly, many congregations are unprepared for death. Funerals are hastily assembled, pastors are unsure how to shepherd grieving families, and theological confusion abounds about what happens after death. The local church must reclaim its role as a community that walks with people from cradle to grave, bearing witness to eternal truths.

One powerful way churches can disciple members in this area is by preaching and teaching on death regularly — not just at funerals or in reaction to tragedies. Scripture is full of truths about mortality, judgment, resurrection, and eternity.

The Psalms teach us to number our days; Ecclesiastes reminds us that the day of death is better than the day of birth because it makes us consider our end. Jesus often spoke of death, not to create fear, but to point to the life found in Him.

Churches can offer seminars or small groups on end-of-life preparation. These should include practical help — writing a will, planning a funeral — but more importantly, they should frame death in light of the gospel. Such gatherings remind people that their identity in Christ extends beyond the grave and that preparing to die well is an act of love for those they leave behind. Pastors must also be trained in pastoral care for the dying.

Visiting the terminally ill, praying with the dying, comforting families, are sacred tasks. A ministry of presence — sitting quietly at a bedside, reading Scripture, singing hymns — is sometimes more powerful than a thousand sermons. These moments are where theology is tangible, and the hope of resurrection becomes more than a doctrine: it becomes the anchor of the soul.

Creating a culture of eternal perspective

Ultimately, dying well is not just a private achievement but a communal formation. The church must be a place where death is not hidden away or sanitized but faced with hope. When churches regularly speak of heaven, of the return of Christ, and of the joy of seeing the Lord face-to-face, they create a culture that helps people live — and die — in light of eternity. Such a culture fosters mission.

Those who are not afraid to die are not afraid to live boldly. When believers know their eternal destiny is secure, they are free to pour themselves out for others, to serve sacrificially, and to take risks for the sake of the gospel. In this way, dying well is not the end of faithfulness — it is its crown.

Confronting fear with faith

For many believers, the greatest obstacle to dying well is not the physical process of death, but the fear of it. This fear can take many forms — fear of suffering, of being forgotten, of leaving loved ones behind, or of facing judgment.

These fears are natural, but they are not ultimate. The gospel speaks directly to each one. The fear of suffering is answered in the presence of Christ, who has promised never to leave or forsake His people. Paul declares in 2 Corinthians 4:16, *"Though outwardly we are wasting away, yet inwardly we are being renewed day by day."* The physical body may decline, but the inner life of the believer grows more radiant with the presence of the Holy Spirit. Jesus does not remove all suffering from His followers, but He sanctifies it, giving it purpose and redeeming it through His own suffering.

The fear of being forgotten is confronted by the eternal memory of God. Even if earthly recognition fades, the names of God's children are written in the Book of Life. The psalmist prays, *"You have kept count of my tossings; put my tears in your bottle — are they not in your book?"* (Psalm 56:8). Every struggle, every sorrow, every act of faithfulness — none are lost to the Father.

For those afraid of leaving loved ones behind, the gospel offers a deep assurance: our God is not only our Shepherd but theirs. We may not be able to remain with our children, our spouse, or our friends, but the One who loves them more than we ever could, will never leave them. Entrusting our loved ones to God's care is one of the final acts of faith. It mirrors the surrender which Jesus made on the cross: *"Father, into your hands I commit my spirit"* (Luke 23:46).

And the fear of judgment? It is answered in the cross. *"There is now no condemnation for those who are in Christ Jesus."* (Rom. 8:1). Christians do not die wondering if they were good enough to make it to heaven. They die resting in the finished work of Christ. The one who trusts in Him has already passed from death to life. Judgment becomes a doorway into joy, not terror.

Cultivating peace through the Psalms

As believers approach death, many find profound comfort in the Psalms. This is no accident. The Psalms give language to every human emotion — joy, despair, hope, sorrow — and they root those emotions in the reality of God's faithfulness.

From the earliest days of the church, the Psalms have been the songs of the dying. Psalm 23 is especially beloved: *"Even though I walk through the valley of the shadow of death, I will fear no evil, for you are with me."* This psalm does not deny the reality of death's valley, but it transforms it. It is a place of shadows, not substance, because the true sting of death has been removed. Jesus walked through the valley before us and now walks with us in it.

Psalm 27 echoes the same assurance: *"The Lord is my light and my salvation – whom shall I fear?"* In moments of weakness, when bodies fail and minds grow dim, the Psalms remind believers that their confidence does not rest in their own strength but in the steadfast love of the Lord. Many Christians have requested Psalm 121 be read on their deathbed: *"I lift up my eyes to the mountains – where does my help come from? My help comes from the Lord, the Maker of heaven and earth."*

These sacred songs become lifelines to the dying soul. They are not merely poetic; they are promises in verse. Even when a dying Christian cannot speak, the Psalms often remain embedded deep in memory. Their cadence and rhythm, forged over a lifetime of worship, rise up when all else fades. Families and pastors who read or sing the Psalms to the dying participate in a holy ministry, offering spiritual oxygen in the final breaths of life.

Finishing the race with grace

Dying well is not about orchestrating the perfect end. It is about remaining faithful to Christ until the end. Some believers pass away peacefully in their sleep. Others endure long, painful illnesses. Some die surrounded by loved ones; others pass alone in hospital rooms. The circumstances vary, but the invitation is the same: finish the race with grace.

The Christian view of death is not morbid. It is hopeful. It is not a denial of grief, but a transformation of it. Believers grieve, but *"not as others do who have no hope."* (1 Thessalonians 4:13). This hope empowers them to die well—not with arrogance, but with assurance; not with bravado, but with blessed confidence in the One who holds the keys to death and Hades.

To die well is to die with Christ's words on our lips: *"It is finished."* Not because we have done everything perfectly, but because He has. The Christian's last act is not to impress God but to rest in Him. We finish our earthly journey not by clinging to life, but by releasing it into the hands of the One who gave it.

And in that release, a new chapter begins—not an end, but a glorious continuation. For those in Christ, death is not a wall but a door. The life to come is not vague or shadowy but vibrant and real. The Christian does not pass into oblivion, but into the presence of the Lord. *"To be away from the body is to be at home with the Lord."* (2 Corinthians 5:8).

Conclusion: The church that teaches its people to die

A healthy church teaches its members how to live—and how to die. It does not shy away from the reality of death, nor does it pretend it can be avoided. Instead, it speaks truthfully, compassionately, and confidently about the journey that awaits every believer.

Pastors and elders have a sacred duty to shepherd their flocks through the valley of the shadow of death. They must preach the resurrection not only on Easter Sunday but in hospital rooms and funeral homes. They must remind God's people that the grave is not the end, that Jesus has gone before them, and that He will come again to make all things new.

When Christians prepare to die well—spiritually, emotionally, relationally, and practically—they glorify God. They love their families. They bless their church. They witness to the world. And they enter eternity not as strangers to God, but as sons and daughters coming home.

May we be such a people. May we die well—not by accident or avoidance, but by grace. May our deaths, like our lives, be testimonies to the mercy and majesty of the One who conquered death, and who now says to each of His own: *"Well done, good and faithful servant… enter into the joy of your Lord."*

17. UNTIL HE COMES: PERSEVERANCE, MISSION, AND THE HOPE OF GLORY

The Christian life is lived in the tension between what is and what is to come. We have tasted the first fruits of salvation, but the full harvest awaits the return of Christ. We live in the "now" of redemption but long for the "not yet" of resurrection glory.

The apostle Paul expresses this dual reality when he writes, *"But our citizenship is in heaven. And we eagerly await a Saviour from there, the Lord Jesus Christ."* (Philippians 3:20). This eager anticipation of Christ's return shapes every aspect of the believer's life — it fuels perseverance, ignites mission, and anchors our hope in the glory to come.

The call to perseverance in a world of trials

One of the most consistent themes in the New Testament is the exhortation to persevere. The Christian life is not a sprint but a marathon, a lifelong journey marked by faithfulness, endurance, and patient hope. The author of Hebrews encourages believers, *"Let us run with perseverance the race marked out for us, fixing our eyes on Jesus, the pioneer and perfecter of faith."* (Hebrews 12:1-2). This call to persevere is not rooted in self-reliance or sheer willpower, but in the sustaining grace of Christ and the certainty of His return.

Perseverance assumes opposition. The New Testament never hides the fact that the road of discipleship is marked with trials, temptations, and tribulations. Jesus Himself said in John 16:33, *"In this world you will have trouble. But take heart! I have overcome the world."*

Peter, likewise, encourages suffering Christians to remain steadfast, knowing that *"the God of all grace... will himself restore you and make you strong, firm and steadfast."* (1 Peter 5:10). Suffering and affliction are not detours from the path of glory — they are often the means by which we are prepared for it.

The hope of glory fuels perseverance. *"Therefore we do not lose heart... For our light and momentary troubles are achieving for us an eternal glory that far outweighs them all."* (2 Corinthians 4:16-17). It is only in the context of eternal perspective that we can regard present hardships as *"light and momentary."* Apart from this hope, suffering might seem pointless and cruel. But in Christ, every trial is purposeful, every pain is pregnant with promise, and every sorrow will one day be turned to joy.

Mission in the meantime: living as witnesses

Waiting for Christ is not passive. It is not a holding pattern in which the church marks time until the trumpet sounds. Rather, it is an active, purposeful, mission-driven life. The parables of Jesus are filled with images of servants waiting for their master — not lounging in idleness, but working diligently, managing their resources, and being faithful stewards of what has been entrusted to them (Matthew 25:14-30).

Jesus made the church's mission plain: *"Go and make disciples of all nations."* (Matthew 28:19). Until He returns, we are to proclaim the gospel, baptize new believers, and teach them to obey all that Christ has commanded. The return of Christ does not diminish the urgency of mission — it heightens it. *"Night is coming, when no one can work."* (John 9:4), Jesus said. The time is short, the fields are ripe for harvest, and we have been commissioned as workers in the vineyard.

Paul captures this sense of urgency when he writes, *"Since, then, we know what it is to fear the Lord, we try to persuade others... Christ's love compels us... We are therefore Christ's ambassadors, as though God were making his appeal through us."* (2 Corinthians 5:11,14,20).

The hope of Christ's return is not an escape hatch from the world, but a motivator to engage it with passion, love, and boldness. We are ambassadors of a kingdom that is coming, bearing witness to a King who reigns and will return in glory. This forward-looking mission is also infused with compassion. We long for the return of Christ, not only for our own vindication and joy, but for the salvation of the lost.

Peter reminds his readers in 2 Peter 3:9 that the apparent delay of Christ's return is not slowness but mercy: *"He is patient with you, not wanting anyone to perish, but everyone to come to repentance."* This means our mission is urgent, but also patient. We speak the truth, call people to repentance, and do so with gentleness and respect (1 Peter 3:15), knowing that the Spirit is at work through our witness.

A hope that anchors the soul

The world in which we live is marked by uncertainty, upheaval, and decay. Political systems falter, economies tremble, and the very earth groans under the weight of sin and brokenness. Against this backdrop, the hope of Christ's return and the consummation of God's kingdom is not just a theological doctrine — it is the anchor of the Christian soul. As the writer to the Hebrews declares, *"We have this hope as an anchor for the soul, firm and secure."* (Hebrews 6:19).

This is not wishful thinking. Christian hope is not rooted in vague optimism or the mere desire for things to improve. It is anchored in the promises of God, sealed by the resurrection of Jesus Christ, and guaranteed by the indwelling of the Holy Spirit.

Paul reminds the believers in Rome, *"Hope does not put us to shame, because God's love has been poured out into our hearts through the Holy Spirit."* (Romans 5:5). Our hope is not merely that things will get better — it is the confident expectation that God will complete what He has begun.

This hope enables believers to live with endurance in the present and with confidence about the future. When we see injustice go unpunished, we remember that the Judge of all the earth will do right. When we see suffering and death, we cling to the promise of resurrection and restoration.

When we feel weak and inadequate, we rest in the assurance that Christ's power is made perfect in our weakness and that our labour in the Lord is never in vain (1 Corinthians 15:58).

Living in light of the end

The New Testament repeatedly calls Christians to live in light of the return of Christ—not in fear or paranoia, but in readiness and holiness. *"The end of all things is near. Therefore, be alert and of sober mind so that you may pray."* (1 Peter 4:7). This eschatological awareness doesn't lead to apathy or detachment from the world, but to deeper engagement in prayer, love, service, and watchfulness.

To live in light of the end means to evaluate our priorities, re-examine our pursuits, and realign our lives with the purposes of God. In Matthew 24:44, Jesus warned His disciples to be ready, *"because the Son of Man will come at an hour when you do not expect him."* That readiness is marked not by speculation or anxiety, but by faithfulness. It is expressed in simple obedience: caring for the hungry, forgiving enemies, loving our neighbours, stewarding our time and resources, and building lives that reflect the character and mission of Christ.

Holiness is another key feature of this eschatological mindset. The apostle John writes, *"All who have this hope in him purify themselves, just as he is pure."* (1 John 3:3). The hope of seeing Christ face to face motivates moral transformation. We long to be found faithful, not out of fear of rejection, but out of love for the One who has saved us. Our sanctification is both a response to His grace and a preparation for His glory.

In 1 Thessalonians 1:9-10, the apostle Paul captures this dynamic beautifully when he describes believers as those *"who have turned to God from idols to serve the living and true God, and to wait for his Son from heaven."* Our posture is both active and expectant: we serve and we wait; we labour and we hope.

Community shaped by future glory

The church, as the gathered people of God, is called to embody this eschatological vision together. We are not individuals preparing for heaven—we are a whole people being shaped into the likeness of Christ as a foretaste of the kingdom to come.

Paul describes the church as *"the pillar and foundation of the truth."* (1 Timothy 3:15), and a community where *"the manifold wisdom of God should be made known... to the rulers and authorities in the heavenly realms."* (Ephesians 3:10). This means our life together has cosmic significance. As a community of hope, the church points forward to the day when *"there will be no more death or mourning or crying or pain."* (Revelation 21:4). Our worship, our fellowship, our service to the poor, our proclamation of the gospel — all these are glimpses of the kingdom breaking into the present age. We live now as citizens of heaven, even as we await the full unveiling of that reality.

This communal dimension of hope also means that we carry one another's burdens, remind one another of the promises of God, and exhort one another to faithfulness. Hebrews urges believers, *"Let us hold unswervingly to the hope we profess, for he who promised is faithful. And let us consider how we may spur one another on toward love and good deeds."* (Hebrews 10:23-24). Hope is not merely personal — it is ecclesial. It is nourished and sustained in the context of shared life in Christ.

The Table of the Lord and the tension of the *"Now and not yet"*

Nowhere is the tension between the present and the future more vividly displayed than in the celebration of the Lord's Supper.

In Matthew 26:29, when Jesus instituted the meal, He did so with the cross in full view, yet with His future kingdom also clearly in mind: *"I tell you, I will not drink of this fruit of the vine from now on until that day when I drink it new with you in my Father's kingdom."* When we eat the bread and drink the cup, we are proclaiming the Lord's death until He comes (1 Corinthians 11:26).

Here is the mystery and the beauty: we look back to the finished work of Christ on the cross, and we look forward to the marriage supper of the Lamb (Revelation 19:9). The table becomes a space where time collapses — past, present, and future converge in the body and blood of Jesus. We are nourished in the present by the grace of a finished redemption and the promise of a final restoration.

But this meal is not just a memorial or a foretaste—it is a means of grace that shapes how we live now. It binds us together as the body of Christ. It confronts us with our need for repentance. It awakens in us a longing for the day when faith will become sight and all things will be made new. It is a call to live in light of what we are celebrating and anticipating. In 1 Corinthians 11:27, Paul reminds us that we must not partake in this supper *"in an unworthy manner"* for the table is sacred. It is a sanctuary of hope, a symbol of unity, and a summons to holiness.

Mission between the times

Living in the *"now and not yet"* also places the church firmly in the stream of mission. We are not waiting passively for Christ to return. We are ambassadors of reconciliation, heralds of good news, builders of communities that reflect the kingdom of God. Jesus declared, *"This gospel of the kingdom will be preached in the whole world... and then the end will come."* (Matthew 24:14). Our missionary task is not a prelude to the kingdom—it is the outworking of the kingdom in real time.

The church is not a bunker where we hide until Jesus comes. We are a city on a hill, a light to the nations, salt of the earth. Our hope should fuel our urgency. Knowing that history is heading toward consummation ought to compel us to make disciples of all nations, to pursue justice, to extend mercy, and to proclaim Christ crucified and risen.

This is why in 2 Corinthians 4:8–10, Paul can speak of suffering and mission in the same breath. *"We are hard pressed on every side, but not crushed; perplexed, but not in despair... always carrying in our body the death of Jesus, so that the life of Jesus may also be revealed in our body."* The suffering church is not a defeated church. She is the suffering servant's bride, sharing in His afflictions as she announces His victory. Hope and mission are inseparably joined. The surety of Christ's return and the glory that awaits us embolden us to press on with joy and perseverance, knowing that our labour is not in vain. As we live in the overlap of the ages, we refuse to retreat or resign. We engage. We serve. We speak. We love.

The benediction of hope

Paul's closing words to the Romans ring as a fitting benediction to the Christian life lived *"until He comes"*: *"May the God of hope fill you with all joy and peace as you trust in him, so that you may overflow with hope by the power of the Holy Spirit."* (Romans 15:13).

To live as people of the new covenant is to live within this benediction. We are people of hope—not naïve, not blind, but confident in the promises of God. Our joy does not come from circumstances but from the Spirit. Our peace does not depend on worldly security but on the sovereignty of our Lord.

We live now with a joy that is often mingled with tears, a peace that often defies reason, and a hope that is rooted not in what we see, but in the One who has gone before us, who even now is preparing a place for us (John 14:2-3). Our faith is not escapism—it is realism of the highest order. It sees the world as it truly is and clings to the One who has overcome it.

Until He comes, we live by faith. We suffer with hope. We worship with joy. We wait with longing. We labour with love. And we feast at the table, remembering the Lamb who was slain and proclaiming the day when He will return in glory to wipe away every tear, to right every wrong, and to make all things new.

So, we pray with the saints of all ages, in every tongue and tribe and nation: *"Come, Lord Jesus."*

APPENDIX A: FREQUENTLY ASKED QUESTIONS

Do Christians go straight to heaven when they die?

Yes. The consistent witness of the New Testament is that those who die in Christ are immediately ushered into the conscious presence of the Lord. This interim state, often referred to as the *"intermediate state,"* is not the final destination, but it is a state of rest, joy, and communion with Christ.

Paul writes, *"To be away from the body and at home with the Lord."* (2 Corinthians 5:8), and he also affirms, *"I desire to depart and be with Christ, which is better by far."* (Philippians 1:23). Jesus assured the thief on the cross in Luke 23:43, *"Today you will be with me in paradise."* These passages indicate immediate fellowship with Christ after death, not soul sleep or unconscious waiting. However, this state is temporary. The ultimate Christian hope is not to *"go to heaven when we die,"* but to be resurrected bodily and to dwell in the new heavens and new earth when Christ returns.

What happens to the body after death?

The body returns to dust (Genesis 3:19), subject to decay and death. Whether it is through burial, cremation, or natural decomposition, the physical body ceases to function and is laid aside. But this is not the end.

The hope of the gospel includes the resurrection of the body. At Christ's return, *"the dead will be raised imperishable"* (1 Cor. 15:52), and the mortal will be clothed with immortality. Our current bodies are like *"seeds"* which are sown in weakness but raised in glory (1 Corinthians 15:42-44). The resurrection body will be transformed, spiritual, imperishable, and glorified—yet still recognizably us, just as resurrected body of Jesus was able to be recognised as Him.

Will we recognize our loved ones in heaven?

Yes. There is every indication in Scripture that personal identity continues after death and that we will recognize one another in the age to come.

At the Mount of Transfiguration, Peter recognized Moses and Elijah (Matthew 17:1-3), even though he had never met them. This points to the reality of personal identity and recognition. Paul speaks of being reunited with believers and presenting them before Christ (1 Thessalonians 2:19; 2 Corinthians 1:14). The emotional and relational bonds of this life are not erased in the new creation—they are transformed and perfected in love.

What is "soul sleep," and is it biblical?

"Soul sleep" is the view that believers, after death, enter a state of unconscious sleep until the resurrection. This idea is held by some groups, but it is not supported by the overall teaching of Scripture.

While death is sometimes described as "sleep" (e.g., John 11:11; 1 Thessalonians 4:13), this is a metaphor for the body's appearance in death, not the condition of the soul. As noted earlier, the biblical witness is that believers are consciously with the Lord after death. Jesus' statement to the thief on the cross – *"Today you will be with me in paradise"* – would make little sense if soul sleep were true.

"Soul sleep" fails to reckon with the richness of biblical imagery about life after death and weakens the immediacy of comfort for those who mourn in Christ.

What about near-death experiences?

Near-death experiences (NDEs) are reports from people who were clinically dead or close to death and then revived. Many describe seeing light, encountering beings, experiencing peace, or even seeing heaven or hell.

While these accounts can be powerful, they are not authoritative. Scripture, not personal experience, must always shape our understanding of death and the afterlife. NDEs may reflect real experiences, but they are subjective, often inconsistent, and may be influenced by cultural, psychological, or spiritual factors.

Deuteronomy 29:29 reminds us, *"The secret things belong to the Lord."* We must resist the temptation to build doctrines on unverifiable experiences. God has told us all we need to know in His Word.

Is cremation biblical?

The Bible does not prescribe a specific method for handling human remains. Burial is more common in biblical times (e.g., Abraham, Jacob, and Jesus were all buried), but cremation is not forbidden. The focus of Scripture is on respect for the body, not the method of its disposal.

God's power to resurrect does not depend on whether a body is intact. Ecclesiastes 12:7 tells us that from dust we came, and to dust we shall return. Whether a body is buried, cremated, lost at sea, or destroyed in a fire, God will restore it in resurrection glory. What matters is the hope of the resurrection, not the form of the grave.

What happens to infants and young children who die?

This question is one of the most sensitive for grieving parents. The Bible does not give a comprehensive doctrinal answer, but several principles offer comfort:

- God is just, merciful, and compassionate. *"Will not the Judge of all the earth do right?"* (Genesis 18:25)
- David, after the death of his infant son, said, *"I will go to him, but he will not return to me."* (2 Samuel 12:23), suggesting an expectation of reunion.
- Jesus welcomed children and spoke of their place in the kingdom of God (Mark 10:14).
- Salvation is by grace, not by mental assent or conscious faith alone. God may apply Christ's redemption to infants and those unable to believe in the same way as adults.

Many theologians affirm the salvation of infants who die, not based on innocence (for all inherit original sin), but on God's sovereign grace.

Can the dead communicate with the living?

No. Scripture strictly forbids any attempt to consult or try and communicate with the dead (Deut. 18:10-12; Isaiah 8:19). This includes practices such as séances, mediums, and spiritualism. These practices open the door to deception and spiritual danger.

The story of the rich man and Lazarus in Luke 16 clearly shows a great chasm between the dead and the living that cannot be crossed. The dead are not permitted to return and give messages to the living. Our hope and guidance must come from God's Word, not from alleged voices beyond the grave.

What is the difference between heaven and the new heavens and new earth?

Heaven as it exists now is the intermediate state—the place where believers go to be with Christ after death. It is real, joyful, and glorious. But it is not the final destination.

The final state is the new heavens and new earth (Rev. 21:1-5), where heaven comes to earth, and God dwells with His people forever. It is not a disembodied spiritual realm but a restored, physical, eternal creation—free from sin, death, and sorrow. In other words, Christians do not hope to escape the world forever—we await its transformation.

Will animals be in the new creation?

The Bible does not give a detailed answer, but there are hints that animals will be present in the new heavens and new earth. Isaiah 11 and 65 speak of animals in the renewed creation, living in peace: *"The wolf will live with the lamb... and a little child will lead them."* (Isaiah 11:6). Creation itself *"waits in eager expectation for the children of God to be revealed"* and *"will be liberated from its bondage to decay."* (Romans 8:19-21). Since animals are part of God's good creation, it is not unreasonable to believe they may share in that renewal. Whether individual pets will be resurrected is uncertain—but God is good, and His new creation will lack nothing that brings joy and completeness.

What about hell? Is it eternal?

Jesus spoke more about hell than anyone else in the Bible. He described it as a place of separation, regret, and judgment (e.g., Matthew 25:41–46; Mark 9:43–48). Revelation calls it the *"lake of fire"* and *"second death"* (Revelation 20:14).

The traditional Christian view is that hell is eternal, conscious separation from God. This is not due to God's cruelty, but His justice. Those who reject God's grace bear the consequences of their sin eternally. It is a sobering doctrine, meant not to satisfy curiosity but to inspire repentance and awe at God's mercy.

Some Christians have explored various different alternatives like annihilationism or conditional immortality, which hold that the wicked cease to exist after judgment. While these are attempts to reconcile justice and mercy, they remain minority positions and face significant biblical challenges.

Should Christians fear death?

In one sense, death is still an enemy (1 Corinthians 15:26). It separates us from loved ones and brings grief. It is a reminder of the Fall and our frailty. But for those in Christ, death has lost its sting (1 Corinthians 15:55). We do not face condemnation, but communion with our risen Lord. Paul could say, *"To live is Christ and to die is gain."* (Philippians 1:21). The believer walks through the valley of the shadow of death with the Good Shepherd (Psalm 23:4).

1 Peter 1:3 tells us that the fear of death has been replaced with a living hope. We do not deny the sorrow of death—but we face it with faith, confidence, and peace.

Will we still be ourselves after the resurrection?

Yes. The resurrection body is a transformed version of our current self, not a replacement. Just as Jesus' risen body was glorified yet recognizably Him (with scars, a voice, the ability to eat and be touched), so will ours be.

Paul uses the analogy of a seed becoming a plant (1 Corinthians 15:35-44). There is continuity and discontinuity. Our memories, personalities, and uniqueness are preserved and perfected in holiness. We will not become generic spirits—we will still be ourselves, fully redeemed.

Can we pray for the dead?

Scripture never commands or commends prayer for the dead. Once a person dies, their eternal destiny is fixed (Hebrews 9:27). There is no such thing as purgatory or post-mortem opportunity for repentance according to the Bible.

Some Christian traditions have developed prayers for the dead, but this is rooted more in tradition than in Scripture. The Protestant Reformation rightly rejected this whole practice as unnecessary and unbiblical. Our responsibility is to pray for the living, proclaim the gospel, and leave the dead to the just and merciful judgment of God.

How should we prepare for our own death?

Spiritually, we prepare by trusting in Jesus Christ, walking in repentance, and living with the assurance of salvation. *"Teach us to number our days,"* the psalmist prays, *"that we may gain a heart of wisdom."* (Psalm 90:12).

Practically, we prepare by speaking with loved ones, making our desires known, arranging our affairs, and ensuring our hope in Christ is clearly expressed in our lives and deaths. We are called to live as those who are ready to die, and to die as those who are ready to live again.

APPENDIX B: KEY BIBLICAL TERMS

This appendix provides brief theological and pastoral definitions for key terms used throughout the book. These terms are often misunderstood and rightly grasping them helps clarify Christian hope in life, death, and eternity.

Afterlife

The general term for existence beyond physical death. In Christian theology, this includes both the intermediate state (life between death and resurrection) and the final state (eternity in the new heavens and new earth or separation from God). The Bible speaks with clarity and hope about life after death for the believer: immediate presence with Christ, followed by bodily resurrection and eternal life.

Annihilationism

A view held by some Christians that those who are not saved will not suffer eternal conscious punishment but will ultimately be destroyed or cease to exist after judgment. While appealing to modern sensibilities, this view is difficult to reconcile with the weight of biblical teaching on eternal separation from God (e.g., Matthew 25:46; Revelation 14:11).

Bodily resurrection

The Christian belief that at the return of Christ, the bodies of all people will be raised from the dead. For believers, the resurrection body will be imperishable, glorious, and spiritual (1 Corinthians 15:42–44). This hope is rooted in the resurrection of Jesus, who is the *"first fruits of those who have fallen asleep"* (1 Corinthians 15:20). Resurrection is not resuscitation, nor merely spiritual continuation, but the transformation of the physical body into a glorified state.

Eternal Life

Not merely unending existence, but the quality of life in communion with God, both now and forever.

Jesus defined eternal life as knowing the Father and the Son (John 17:3). It begins in the present through faith in Christ and will be perfected in the age to come when believers dwell with God forever (Revelation 21:3-4).

Gehenna

A term used by Jesus to describe the final state of judgment for the wicked (e.g., Matthew 5:22, 10:28). Originally a valley outside Jerusalem associated with idolatry and burning refuse, it became a powerful image of divine judgment. Gehenna is often translated as "hell" and refers not to the intermediate state but to the eternal punishment of the unrighteous after the final judgment.

Glory

In Scripture, "glory" refers to the radiant manifestation of God's presence, beauty, and holiness. For believers, glorification is the final step of salvation, where they are transformed into the likeness of Christ and share in His glory (Romans 8:30; 2 Corinthians 3:18). Glory is the destiny of God's people—to reflect His splendour forever.

Heaven

Heaven refers to both the current dwelling place of God and the intermediate state of believers after death. It is where God's will is perfectly done and where the souls of the redeemed are consciously with Christ (Philippians 1:23). However, the Bible's ultimate focus is not on going to heaven, but on heaven coming to earth in the new creation (Revelation 21:1-5).

Hell

The final place of judgment for those who reject God's salvation. Described in terms of fire, darkness, and separation, hell is the eternal counterpart to the eternal life of the redeemed. Jesus warned repeatedly about its reality. While interpretations of the nature of hell differ, Scripture consistently presents it as the ultimate loss of God's presence and the consequence of unrepented sin (Matthew 25:46; 2 Thessalonians 1:9).

Hades

Often confused with "hell," Hades in the New Testament refers more generally to the realm of the dead—the temporary abode of departed souls. In Luke 16:23, Hades is described as a place of conscious awareness and torment for the unrighteous prior to final judgment. It is distinct from Gehenna, which refers to the final state of punishment.

Immortality

In biblical usage, "immortality" refers to the imperishable nature of the resurrection body (1 Corinthians 15:53-54). While God alone possesses immortality in Himself (1 Timothy 6:16), He grants it to believers through union with Christ. Immortality is not the natural possession of the soul, but a gift of grace through resurrection life.

Intermediate State

The condition of human existence between death and the resurrection. For believers, it is conscious fellowship with Jesus Christ (2 Corinthians 5:8); for unbelievers, it is separation and anticipation of final judgment (Luke 16:22-26). This state is temporary and incomplete, pointing forward to the final consummation of God's plan.

Judgment

Judgment refers to the righteous assessment of people by God. Hebrews 9:27 says, *"People are destined to die once, and after that to face judgment."* There is a particular judgment (immediately after death) and a final judgment at the return of Christ (Revelation 20:11-15). For believers, judgment brings reward for the unrepentant, it confirms separation from God.

Kingdom of God

The rule and reign of God, which broke into human history through Jesus Christ. The kingdom is "already" present in the life of the Church and the ministry of the Spirit, but "not yet" fully manifested until Christ returns (Matt. 6:10; Luke 17:20-21). In eternity, the kingdom will be consummated as God's people dwell with Him in a renewed creation (Revelation 11:15).

Lake of Fire

A symbolic term used in Revelation to describe the final destination of Satan, his angels, and all those not written in the Book of Life (Revelation 20:10, 14-15). It is associated with *"the second death"* and eternal separation from God. The image is drawn from fiery judgment motifs throughout Scripture and underscores the seriousness of rejecting God's grace.

Last things (Eschatology)

The branch of theology concerned with death, judgment, heaven, hell, resurrection, and the return of Christ. Derived from the Greek word *eschatos* ("last"), eschatology explores how God brings His purposes to completion. Christian eschatology is both personal (what happens when I die?) and cosmic (how will history end?). Its goal is not speculation, but preparation and hope.

New creation / new heavens and new earth

The final state of redeemed existence, where God dwells with His people in a restored and glorified cosmos (Isaiah 65:17; Revelation 21:1-5). It is not merely a return to Eden, but a transformation of all things through Christ. Death, pain, and sin are no more. The new creation is the culmination of God's redemptive plan and the true home of every believer.

Paradise

A term used by Jesus in Luke 23:43 (*"Today you will be with me in paradise"*) to describe the blessed state of the righteous dead. Originally a Persian word meaning *"garden,"* it came to represent the place of rest and delight in God's presence. It is sometimes used synonymously with heaven, though it technically refers to the intermediate state before resurrection.

Purgatory

A doctrine held by the Roman Catholic Church describing a post-mortem process of purification for believers who are not yet ready for heaven.

It has no direct support in Scripture and is rejected by Protestant theology. The New Testament teaches that Christ's atonement fully cleanses believers (Hebrews 10:14), and that to be absent from the body is to be present with the Lord (2 Corinthians 5:8).

Resurrection

The core of Christian hope: the raising of the dead in glorified bodies. Jesus' resurrection is both the basis and the pattern for ours. Paul teaches in 1 Corinthians 15:22), that *"in Christ all will be made alive."* The resurrection involves both the just and the unjust (Acts 24:15), but only the redeemed will rise to eternal life.

Salvation

God's gracious deliverance of sinners through the life, death, and resurrection of Jesus Christ. Salvation includes justification (being declared righteous), sanctification (being made holy), and glorification (being perfected in eternity). It is by grace, through faith—not by works—and secures eternal life and resurrection hope (Ephesians 2:8-9; Romans 8:30).

Second coming (Parousia)

The promised return of Jesus Christ in glory to judge the living and the dead, raise the righteous, and establish His eternal kingdom. The New Testament urges believers to live in readiness: *"The Lord himself will come down from heaven... and the dead in Christ will rise first."* (1 Thessalonians 4:16). The second coming marks the climax of history and the beginning of the new creation.

Sheol

The Hebrew term for the realm of the dead, used frequently in the Old Testament. It encompasses both the righteous and the wicked before the fuller revelation of the afterlife in the New Testament. Sheol is often portrayed as a shadowy existence, lacking the clarity and hope of later eschatological teaching. The New Testament equivalent is *"Hades."*

Soul

The immaterial aspect of human beings, often synonymous with the *"self"* or *"life."* Biblically, humans are both body and soul, created in the image of God (Genesis 2:7; Matthew 10:28). At death, the soul separates from the body but will be reunited with it in the resurrection. The soul is not inherently immortal in Greek philosophical terms but is preserved by God through grace.

Theodicy

The defence of God's goodness and justice in the face of suffering and evil. In discussions of death and dying, theodicy asks: *"If God is good and all-powerful, why do people die?"* While Scripture does not give exhaustive answers, it points to human sin, the Fall, and the cross of Christ as the ultimate response to evil. God has entered into suffering and conquered death through Jesus.

"The Last Enemy"

A term used in 1 Corinthians 15:26 to describe death. Though defeated at the cross and resurrection, death will be finally destroyed at Christ's return. This reminds us that death is not natural or benign—it is the enemy of life, introduced by sin. But it is also the defeated enemy, and its days are numbered.

APPENDIX C: KEY BIBLE PASSAGES

This appendix collects key Bible passages that have shaped Christian teaching on death, the intermediate state, and the resurrection of the dead, and eternal life.

Genesis 3:17–19

To Adam he said, "Because you listened to your wife and ate fruit from the tree about which I commanded you, 'You must not eat from it,' cursed is the ground because of you; through painful toil you will eat food from it all the days of your life.

It will produce thorns and thistles for you, and you will eat the plants of the field. By the sweat of your brow, you will eat your food until you return to the ground, since from it you were taken; for dust you are and to dust you will return."

Job 19:25–27

I know that my redeemer lives, and that in the end he will stand on the earth. And after my skin has been destroyed, yet in my flesh I will see God; I myself will see him with my own eyes – I, and not another. How my heart yearns within me!

Psalm 23:4–6

Even though I walk through the darkest valley, I will fear no evil, for you are with me; your rod and your staff, they comfort me. You prepare a table before me in the presence of my enemies. You anoint my head with oil; my cup overflows. Surely your goodness and love will follow me all the days of my life, and I will dwell in the house of the Lord forever.

Psalm 49:15

But God will redeem me from the realm of the dead; he will surely take me to himself.

Psalm 116:15

Precious in the sight of the Lord is the death of his faithful servants.

Isaiah 25:7-9

On this mountain he will destroy the shroud that enfolds all peoples, the sheet that covers all nations; he will swallow up death forever. The Sovereign Lord will wipe away the tears from all faces; he will remove his people's disgrace from all the earth. The Lord has spoken. In that day they will say, "Surely this is our God; we trusted in him, and he saved us. This is the Lord, we trusted in him; let us rejoice and be glad in his salvation."

Isaiah 26:19

But your dead will live, Lord; their bodies will rise – let those who dwell in the dust wake up and shout for joy – your dew is like the dew of the morning; the earth will give birth to her dead.

Daniel 12:2-3

Multitudes who sleep in the dust of the earth will awake: some to everlasting life, others to shame and everlasting contempt. Those who are wise will shine like the brightness of the heavens, and those who lead many to righteousness, like the stars for ever and ever.

Matthew 10:28

Do not be afraid of those who kill the body but cannot kill the soul. Rather, be afraid of the One who can destroy both soul and body in hell.

Matthew 22:31-32

But about the resurrection of the dead – have you not read what God said to you, "I am the God of Abraham, the God of Isaac, and the God of Jacob"? He is not the God of the dead but of the living.

Matthew 25:31-34, 46

When the Son of Man comes in his glory, and all the angels with him, he will sit on his glorious throne. All the nations will be gathered before him... Then the King will say to those on his right, "Come, you who are blessed by my Father; take your inheritance, the kingdom prepared for you since the creation of the world." ... Then they will go away to eternal punishment, but the righteous to eternal life.

Luke 16:22-26

The time came when the beggar died and the angels carried him to Abraham's side. The rich man also died and was buried. In Hades, where he was in torment, he looked up and saw Abraham far away, with Lazarus by his side.

So he called to him, "Father Abraham, have pity on me... I am in agony in this fire." But Abraham replied, "Between us and you a great chasm has been set in place, so that those who want to go from here to you cannot, nor can anyone cross over from there to us."

Luke 23:42-43

Then he said, "Jesus, remember me when you come into your kingdom." Jesus answered him, "Truly I tell you, today you will be with me in paradise."

John 5:28-29

A time is coming when all who are in their graves will hear his voice and come out – those who have done what is good will rise to live, and those who have done what is evil will rise to be condemned.

John 11:25-26

Jesus said to her, "I am the resurrection and the life. The one who believes in me will live, even though they die; and whoever lives by believing in me will never die. Do you believe this?"

John 14:1-3

Do not let your hearts be troubled. You believe in God; believe also in me. My Father's house has many rooms; if that were not so, would I have told you that I am going there to prepare a place for you? And if I go and prepare a place for you, I will come back and take you to be with me that you also may be where I am.

Acts 24:15

I have the same hope in God as these men themselves have, that there will be a resurrection of both the righteous and the wicked.

Romans 6:5–8

For if we have been united with him in a death like his, we will certainly also be united with him in a resurrection like his... Now if we died with Christ, we believe that we will also live with him.

Romans 8:10–11

But if Christ is in you, then even though your body is subject to death because of sin, the Spirit gives life because of righteousness. And if the Spirit of him who raised Jesus from the dead is living in you, he who raised Christ from the dead will also give life to your mortal bodies because of his Spirit who lives in you.

Romans 8:18–23

I consider that our present sufferings are not worth comparing with the glory that will be revealed in us... We know that the whole creation has been groaning as in the pains of childbirth right up to the present time. Not only so, but we ourselves... groan inwardly as we wait eagerly for our adoption to sonship, the redemption of our bodies.

1 Corinthians 15:12–26

But if it is preached that Christ has been raised from the dead, how can some of you say that there is no resurrection of the dead?... If Christ has not been raised, your faith is futile; you are still in your sins...

But Christ has indeed been raised from the dead, the first fruits of those who have fallen asleep... The last enemy to be destroyed is death.

1 Corinthians 15:42–44, 51–55

So will it be with the resurrection of the dead. The body that is sown is perishable, it is raised imperishable... it is sown a natural body, it is raised a spiritual body...

Listen, I tell you a mystery: We will not all sleep, but we will all be changed...

The perishable must clothe itself with the imperishable... then the saying that is written will come true: "Death has been swallowed up in victory."

2 Corinthians 4:14-18

We know that the one who raised the Lord Jesus from the dead will also raise us with Jesus and present us with you to himself... Therefore, we do not lose heart. Though outwardly we are wasting away, yet inwardly we are being renewed day by day... So, we fix our eyes not on what is seen, but on what is unseen.

2 Corinthians 5:1-10

For we know that if the earthly tent we live in is destroyed, we have a building from God... Meanwhile we groan, longing to be clothed instead with our heavenly dwelling... We are confident, I say, and would prefer to be away from the body and at home with the Lord.

Philippians 1:21-23

For to me, to live is Christ and to die is gain... I desire to depart and be with Christ, which is better by far.

Philippians 3:20-21

But our citizenship is in heaven. And we eagerly await a Savior from there, the Lord Jesus Christ, who... will transform our lowly bodies so that they will be like his glorious body.

1 Thessalonians 4:13-18

Brothers and sisters, we do not want you to be uninformed about those who sleep in death... For the Lord himself will come down from heaven... and the dead in Christ will rise first... And so, we will be with the Lord forever.

1 Thessalonians 5:9-10

For God did not appoint us to suffer wrath but to receive salvation through our Lord Jesus Christ. He died for us so that, whether we are awake or asleep, we may live together with him.

2 Timothy 4:6-8

The time for my departure is near. I have fought the good fight, I have finished the race, I have kept the faith... Now there is in store for me the crown of righteousness, which the Lord... will award to me on that day.

Hebrews 9:27-28

Just as people are destined to die once, and after that to face judgment, so Christ was sacrificed once to take away the sins of many... he will appear a second time, not to bear sin, but to bring salvation to those who are waiting for him.

Revelation 1:17-18

Do not be afraid. I am the First and the Last. I am the Living One; I was dead, and now look, I am alive for ever and ever! And I hold the keys of death and Hades.

Revelation 7:16-17

Never again will they hunger; never again will they thirst... For the Lamb at the centre of the throne will be their shepherd... and God will wipe away every tear from their eyes.

Revelation 20:12-15

And I saw the dead, great and small, standing before the throne... The dead were judged according to what they had done... Anyone whose name was not found written in the book of life was thrown into the lake of fire.

Revelation 21:1-5

Then I saw a new heaven and a new earth... I heard a loud voice from the throne saying, "Look! God's dwelling place is now among the people... He will wipe every tear from their eyes. There will be no more death or mourning or crying or pain, for the old order of things has passed away." He who was seated on the throne said, "I am making everything new!"

www.ingramcontent.com/pod-product-compliance
Lightning Source LLC
Chambersburg PA
CBHW070759040426
42333CB00060B/1223